Better French 2

Past and Imperfect Tenses

Studymates

Algebra: Basic Algebra Explained
Better English
Better French
Better French 2
Better German
Better Spanish
British History 1870-1918
Chemistry: chemistry calculations explained
European History
Genetics
Hitler & Nazi Germany
Lenin, Stalin and Communist Russia
Mathematics for adults
Organic Chemistry
Plant Physiology
Poems to Live By
Poetry
Practical Drama
Shakespeare
Social Anthropology
Study skills
The Academic Essay
The English Reformation
The New Science Teacher's Handbook
The War Poets
Understanding Maths
Warfare

Studymates Writers Guides

Kate Walker's 12-Point Guide to Writing Romance
Starting to Write
Writing Crime Fiction
Writing Historical Fiction
Writing Tv Scripts

Studymates Post-Graduate Guides

Your Masters Thesis
Your PhD Thesis

Many other titles in preparation

Better French 2

Past and Imperfect Tenses

The full picture, step-by-step

Monique Jackman
BA (Open), Further Education Teacher's Certificate

www.studymates.co.uk

ISBN: 978-1-84285-094-7

First published in 2007 by Studymates Limited.
PO Box 225, Abergele, LL18 9AY, United Kingdom.

Website: http://www.studymates.co.uk

Typeset by Vikatan Publishing Solutions, Chennai, India
Printed and bound in Great Britain by Baskerville Press

Contents

Preface

Past and Imperfect Tenses
The full picture, step-by-step

When talking about the past: past actions, what happened, what has happened, what has been happening, what did happen, what was happening, what used to happen, or when talking about how people and things were or used to be, and so on, as is the case in English, French uses two past tenses: the perfect (*le passé composé*) and the imperfect (*l'imparfait*). These are the tenses used in everyday conversation, in informal accounts and in letters.

Perfect Past Tenses could be described as a book of 'classroom explanations' on this subject, arguably the most challenging part of the five-year usual standard school course, revised and extended at post-16 level. In my experience, both teenaged and adult learners often initially find this to be a particularly difficult stage. I have also found that once they have absorbed the main differences between the tenses, they can suddenly go backwards and experience another confusing stage, when they find themselves wondering whether everything will ever eventually click into place.

In this book, uses of the two tenses are explained step by step, in a meticulous and systematic fashion and entirely in English. Various suggestions on how to explain the rules are provided. Repetition is deliberate. Following each rule section are examples in English. The different formations are then explained step by step and, together with further examples, the examples given in English in the previous sections are repeated and translated. Parallel translation of all the examples allows students to concentrate fully on the different uses and formations, so that these fall into place and are absorbed as quickly as possible.

The purpose of *BETTER FRENCH 2 Perfect Past Tenses* is to enable students who have reached a certain level in their learning to grasp the different uses of the two past tenses;

to study all their different formations in a methodical way; and to find answers to their questions on the subject, all at their own pace. It is, naturally, always a relief to realise that some French grammar can have a 'full picture,' and I do feel that teachers and students of French would find that a work such as *Perfect Past Tenses*, that offers a full picture of a particular grammatical area, provides a valuable short cut to individuals teaching and learning these past tenses, as well as a handy reference tool thereafter.

Three further past tenses are briefly discussed, primarily for comparison purposes. These are the two past tenses that are also used in conversation, the pluperfect (what had happened) the dreaded subjunctive perfect (more or less untranslatable in English), and the past historic, which replaces the perfect tense mostly in novels and other formal printed texts.

I hope that this book will make some of the problems and worry surrounding its subject-matter a thing of the past!

Monique Jackman
monique.jackman@studymates.co.uk

When to use the Perfect Tense

The word 'perfect' comes from the Latin 'perfectus' and means 'finished' or 'completed.' What is the French for 'I ate,' 'I have eaten,' 'I have been eating' and 'I did eat?' This chapter lists general rules governing use of the perfect tense. Several ways of explaining these are suggested. Unavoidable grey areas are explained in the form of extensions to the rules. A number of examples in English follow each list of rules and each extra rule.

The perfect tense in French is used:

- To translate completed, finished events and actions;
- to say what you or others have done or did;
- to talk about what was done or has been done;
- to express any event which is now complete;
- to refer to something that occurred in the past;
- to say what happened first in a story
- and then what happened next, i.e.
- to list or record successive events in a story;
- to give a series of past actions.

I saw my friend. I have seen my friend. I did see my friend.
You finished the work. You have finished the work. You did finish the work.
She fell. She has fallen. She did fall.
He phoned. He has phoned. He did phone.
We spoke. We have spoken. We did speak.
You ate out? Have you eaten out? Did you eat out?
I read this book twice. I have read this book twice. I did read this book twice.
She had a cold. She has had a cold. She did have a cold.

They went to Paris? Have they gone to Paris? Did they go to Paris?

I took my driving test in 1998. I have taken my driving test. I did take my driving test.

His cat watched the birds. His cat has watched the birds. His cat did watch the birds.

Her dog died? Has her dog died? Did her dog die?

The books fell on the floor. They have fallen on the floor. They did fall on the floor.

There was some noise outside. There has been some noise outside.

The car broke down? Has it broken down? Did it break down?

The letters helped my mother. They have helped my mother. They did help my mother.

The weather changed. It has changed. It did change.

Your friend sent presents? Has your friend sent presents? Did your friend send presents?

The film started late. It has started late. It did start late.

It was a long week. It has been a long week.

They complained. They have complained. They did complain.

Have you apologised? Did you apologise?

Were you born in Provence?

I nearly fell. I did nearly fall.

Prices dropped. Prices have dropped. Prices did drop.

It happened three times. It has happened three times. It did happen three times.

She beat all records. She has beaten all records. She did beat all records.

He broke my heart. He has broken my heart. He did break my heart.

The cat chased the squirrel. The cat has chased the squirrel. The cat did chase the squirrel.

It snowed. It has snowed. It has been snowing. It did snow.

It was necessary to pay in euros.

They became poor? Have they become poor? Did they become poor?

She came, had lunch and read the newspaper.

They went to a restaurant last night, then came home and played chess.

I went to bed at eleven, slept until eight this morning and got up at about nine.

He ate some snails and was so sick the next day that he called the doctor.

He arrived, asked for a coffee, sat down and made a phone call.

I woke up, got up, washed, dressed, went down, had breakfast, and left the house.

The puppies were born this morning, but two died an hour later.

The train appeared in the fog, slowed down, and stopped.

> ➤ Using an expression of time to refer to events and actions that lasted for a fixed period of time does make the meaning clear:

He lived with you for how many years?

We were cold/have been cold all night.

I stayed/did stay in bed for two days.

They lived/did live in Marseilles from 1969 to 2000.

He waited/has waited/did wait twenty minutes.

It was/has been a sad year.

They watched/have watched/did watch television from two to five.

You stayed/did you stay a long time?

It rained/has rained/did rain all week.

They sang/did sing between eight and ten o'clock.

I wrote/did write letters to my English friend for ten years.

The dog was ill the whole weekend.

They defended/did defend their son for a long time.

We cooked/have been cooking/did cook all morning.

The population decreased/has decreased/did decrease over the years.

It caused/has caused/did cause embarrassment for the rest of the weekend.

> ➢ However, a point of reference in time can also be only implied:

It was/has been an expensive holiday.
They had/have had a very happy time.
She was/has been a singer.
He was/has been married.
The party was/has been lovely?
My husband enjoyed his childhood.
She was bored at her aunt's.
She lost/has lost/did lose weight during her illness.
It was/has been an unforgettable experience.
I enjoyed/have enjoyed/did enjoy this last lesson.
They walked/have walked/did walk/have been walking just a little too long.
They have been working really hard.
I have been looking at old photographs.
We have been helping our best friends move house.
He has been reading the newspaper.
They have been talking to their cousins.

> ➢ By extension, the last two rules given above apply when referring to a repeated event of any duration which is definitely limited in time; an action or event repeated a specific number of times over a precise period; and happenings regarded as completed facts:

I had curry several times in that restaurant.
Did you take your driving test three times?
They played together every day last week.
I went to France every year before my marriage.
How many times did they ring today?
She went to the hospital every week for three months.
We wrote several times in December.
My parents thought about us every night last month.
How many times were you late last week?
I saw the film twice and cried each time.
I stirred the sauce regularly for an hour.
She came with us several times in the summer.

We counted the tickets at least three times.
They came every week in November.
He made the most of each weekend to redecorate the kitchen.
She spilled her glass each night.

> ➤ Events in the moral sphere (as well as in the physical and material sphere) are also definite happenings, for example a sudden emotion, feeling or sensation:

Suddenly I was worried.
You were wrong to shout.
She was very cross.
He was embarrassed when she said that.
We were very disappointed to hear the news.
They looked sad.
I needed to talk to my boss immediately.
Have you had/did you have a surprise?
Were you ashamed of your results?
I was very moved when I saw the house.
My son was right to leave.
He got scared.
She wanted to leave everything.
We hoped to the end.
They wanted to see for themselves.
I was staggered.
NOTE: The imperfect tense could equally be used with these last examples (see Chapters Seven and Nine).

> ➤ When new circumstances, new conditions or new situations very suddenly came into being, although not actual actions, these are also considered to be definite, completed occurrences:

I was unexpectedly sleepy at nine.
He was stupid to believe his story.
All of a sudden he was/got cold.
After five the children were/got hungry.
The animals got too hot this summer.

They were very lucky (when they bought their car).
All at once it got foggy.
Then there was a problem.
So, we had to go.
There were many questions (when he finished speaking).
Suddenly there was a scream.
After that the street was quiet.
You trusted him too much.
I was surprised to see them there.
We had to decide.
It became too complicated.

NOTE: It would not be incorrect to use the imperfect tense with most of these last examples (see Chapters Seven and Nine).

> On the other hand, overlapping with some of what is stated above, the perfect tense, when the imperfect tense would also be correct, can be used for style purposes, for stress, to give more <u>vividness</u> *and* <u>immediacy</u> *to the verb*:

The shop assistant was helpful yesterday.
When I was (turned) twenty (I decided to buy a car).
We wanted to make a difference.
That's what she thought.
She fancied going to the cinema.
You were rather naïve.
You looked please (when the phone rang).
Only my father understood my brother.
He looked upset.
It was impossible.
I wanted to speak to the teacher yesterday.
They thought that it would be better.
We wanted to be there.
Was it tiring?
We thought the opposite.
You looked frightened.

> ➤ One simple rule, that is also covered in the rules and examples above, is that <u>whenever</u> the past tense used in English is the compound perfect tense, for example 'they have worked in the garden' or 'they have been working in the garden' (in the sense of started *and* <u>finished</u>), the French perfect tense is needed, *EXCEPT* with two key structures:

1. *The present tense, not a past tense is used in French (see Chapters Six and Thirteen) when the English perfect tense conveys an action that is still continuing and <u>not finished</u> as in the examples below:*

She has been smoking since January.
He has been married for two months.
She has only been here an hour.
How long have you been a vegetarian?
They have been divorced for a few weeks.
We have been working in the garden for twenty minutes.
They have shared a room for two months.
Someone has been knocking on the front door for five minutes.
It has rained for three days.
They have been on a diet for five weeks.
I have been worried since six o'clock.
How long have you known this man?
He has lived here since January.
He has been asleep since five.
She has been irritating her brother since this morning.

2. *The second exception to the rule that the compound perfect tense in English means the perfect tense in French is in the 'to have just done something' key structure, sometimes referred to as the very recent past. To translate the examples below into French, the present tense of 'venir' is used with the main verb in the infinitive (this is explained fully in Chapters Six and Thirteen):*

7

I have just seen the postman.
You have just missed your friend.
She has just finished.
He has just fallen.
We have just asked.
Have you just had a shower?
They have just arrived
I have just been ill.
We have just used the lawn mower.
She has just completed the form.
The dog has just barked.
She has just left.
He has just sent an email.
We have just had a cup of tea.
Have you just washed the dress?

Helping you learn

Progress questions

1. What are the rules governing use of the perfect tense?
2. Check your answer.

Discussion points

1. Discuss rules for use of the perfect tense with fellow students and anyone else interested in the subject.
2. Discuss grey areas, when one of two tenses could be correct.
3. Make comparisons with talking about the past in English.

Practical assignment

1. Write down in English what you did yesterday.
2. Work out which verbs would take the perfect tense in French.
3. Discuss with fellow students and anyone else interested in the subject.

Study tips

1. Read and re-read rules and appropriate examples until you have absorbed the rules.
2. Little and often works well.

2 Formation of the Perfect Tense

One-minute overview

In English, there are four different ways of expressing an action that has taken place, which can often be interchangeable:

- I have cried
- I cried
- I did cry
- I have been crying

In French, there is only one way of translating all four examples – the first: I have cried.

Past participles are needed to form the perfect tense. Chapter Two explains what these are and how to form all four groups.

◼ When talking about something that happened in the past in English, the verb 'to have' and the past participle of the appropriate verb can be used, as in the first of the four examples above. French basically works in the same way: the French perfect tense is a compound tense (composed of two parts/words/verbs). It is formed in the same way for all verbs: the auxiliary verb of either *avoir* or *être* in the present tense and the past participle of the main verb. In order to form the perfect tense, therefore, one must know (or guess) the past participle.

➤ Examples of past participles:

arrived, as in 'I have **arrived**.'
been, as in 'They have **been** silly.'
bought, as in 'What have you **bought**?
cooked, as in 'I have **cooked** the fish.'

died, as in 'She has **died**.'
done, as in 'What have you **done**?'
eaten, as in 'He has **eaten**.'
enjoyed, as in 'We have **enjoyed** the play.'
fallen, as in 'The child has **fallen**.'
finished, as in 'She has **finished**.'
followed, as in 'They have **followed** the soap.'
gone, as in 'She has **gone** to Paris.'
had, as in 'They have **had** a baby.'
kissed, as in 'He has **kissed** them.'
liked, as in 'They have **liked** the show.'
lost, as in 'We have **lost**.'
made, as in 'What have they **made**?'
opened, as in 'I have **opened** the tin.'
played, as in 'I have **played**.'
read, as in 'Have you **read** this book?'
seen, as in 'They have **seen** the film.'
sold, as in 'He has **sold** his bike.'
spent, as in 'I have **spent** too much.'
started, as in 'We have **started**.'
taken, as in 'Who has **taken** the paper?'

> ➤ There are regular and irregular past participles in both English and French. In French, there are three groups of verbs that have regular past participles, as well as a fourth group of verbs that have irregular past participles and no fixed rule governing formation of their past participles.
> ➤ In order to obtain a past participle, the stem of the verb (also known as its root) is needed. To find the stem, the infinitive ending, -*er*, -*ir* or -*re*, is removed.
> ➤ For all -*er* verbs, the -*er* is removed and replaced with -*é*, (there is no change in pronunciation):

Appel**er**:	*Tu as appel**é** ton père?*
	Have you called/did you call your father?
Célébr**er**:	*Ils ont célébr**é** Noël ensemble.*
	They celebrated/have celebrated/did celebrate Christmas together.

Command**er**:	*Elles ont commandé des livres.*
	They ordered/have ordered/did order some books
Démarr**er**:	*Le bus a démarré.*
	The bus has driven/drove/did drive off.
Echou**er**:	*Il a échoué le permis de conduire.*
	He failed/has failed/did fail his driving test.
Emprunt**er**:	*Elle a emprunté mon stylo.*
	She borrowed/has borrowed/did borrow my pen.
Grill**er**:	*J'ai grillé les côtelettes.*
	I grilled/have grilled/did grill the chops.
Habill**er**:	*Tu as habillé le bébé?*
	Have you dressed/did you dress the baby?
Lou**er**:	*Nous avons loué une voiture.*
	We hired/have hired/did hire a car.
Not**er**:	*Tu as noté l'adresse?*
	Have you/did you make a note of the address?
Parrain**er**:	*Ma compagnie a parrainé cette institution charitable deux fois.*
	My company sponsored/has sponsored/did sponsor this charity twice.
Ronfl**er**:	*Vous avez ronflé toute la nuit.*
	You snored/have been snoring/did snore all night.

➤ For most verbs ending in *-ir*, the ending *-ir* becomes *-i*:

Ag**ir**:	*Est-ce qu'ils ont agi à temps?*
	Have they acted/did they act in time?
Avert**ir**:	*Tu as averti le maire?*
	Have you warned/did you warn the mayor?
Bond**ir**:	*J'ai bondi.*
	I went/did go mad.
Fin**ir**:	*Tu as fini?*
	Have you/did you finish?

Fleur**ir**:   *Les roses ont fleur**i** tôt cette année.*
The roses flowered/have flowered/did flower early this year.

Fu**ir**:   *Ils ont fu**i**.*
They ran away/have run away/did run away.

Guér**ir**:   *Il a guér**i**.*
He has been/was cured.

Maigr**ir**:   *Vous avez maigr**i**.*
You have lost/lost/did lose weight.

Obé**ir**:   *Ils ont obé**i**.*
They obeyed/have obeyed/did obey.

Réfléch**ir**:   *Vous avez réfléch**i**?*
Have you thought/did you think about it?

Serv**ir**:   *Est-ce qu'elles ont serv**i** le vin?*
Have they/did they serve the wine?

Sub**ir**:   *Nous avons sub**i** des insultes.*
We received/have received/did receive insults.

> ➤ For some verbs ending in *-re*, the ending *-re* is replaced by *-u*:

Attend**re**:   *Il a attend**u** où?*
Where did he wait?

Batt**re**:   *Il a batt**u** son enfant.*
He hit/has hit/did hit his child.

Descend**re**:   *J'ai descend**u** le plateau.*
I took/have taken/did take the tray downstairs.

Entend**re**:   *Nous avons entend**u** l'alarme.*
We heard/have heard/did hear the alarm.

Fond**re**:   *La glace a fond**u**.*
The ice melted/has melted/did melt.

Mord**re**:   *Elle a mord**u** mon gâteau!*
She bit/has bitten/did bite my cake!

Prétend**re**:   *Elle a prétend**u** être malade.*
She pretended/has pretended/did pretend to be ill.

Rend**re**:	*Est-ce que vous avez rend**u** la clé à ma sœur?*
	Have you/did you give the key back to my sister?
Répand**re**:	*Cela a répand**u** la panique.*
	That caused/has cause/did cause some panic
Répond**re**:	*Ils ont répond**u**?*
	Have they replied/did they reply?
Tond**re**:	*J'ai tond**u** le gazon.*
	I mowed/have mowed/did mow the lawn.
Tord**re**:	*Qui a tord**u** la fourchette?*
	Who bent/has bent/did bend the fork?

> ➤ Unfortunately, just as is the case in English, there are also *many verbs* that do not follow any of the set patterns above and form their past participles differently (these verbs are usually the same common ones that are irregular in the present tense, such as 'to make,' 'to want,' 'to have to'). These forms have to be learned gradually by heart as they occur:

Avoir:	*Ils ont **eu** une surprise.*
	They had/have had a surprise.
Connaître:	*Elle a **connu** mon grand-père.*
	She knew/has known/did know my grandfather.
Coudre:	*J'ai **cousu** tout le matin.*
	I have been sewing/have sewed all morning.
Couvrir:	*On a **couvert** les sandwiches.*
	We covered/have covered/did cover the sandwiches.
Devoir:	*On a **dû** payer.*
	We had/have had to pay.
Etre:	*Vous avez **été** jaloux?*
	Have you been/were you jealous?
Faire:	*Il a **fait** beaucoup de sports.*
	He has done/did a good number of sports.

Falloir:	*Il a __fallu__ céder.*
	We had/have had to give in.
Pleuvoir:	*Il a __plu__ toute la nuit.*
	It rained/has rained/did rain the whole night.
Pouvoir:	*J'ai __pu__ rester.*
	I was/have been able to stay.
Prendre:	*Qu'est-ce qu'elles ont __pris__?*
	What have they taken/did they take?
Prévenir:	*Nous avons __prévenu__ la police.*
	We contacted/have contacted/did contact the police.
Reconnaître:	*J'ai __reconnu__ votre voisin.*
	I recognised/have recognised/did recognise your neighbour.
Rire:	*Ils ont __ri__.*
	They laughed/have laughed/did laugh.
Sourire:	*On a __souri__.*
	We smiled/have smiled/did smile.
Suivre:	*Ils ont __suivi__ le car.*
	They followed/have followed/did follow the coach.
Surprendre:	*Ils ont __surpris__ le voleur.*
	They caught/have caught/did catch the thief red-handed.
Traduire:	*Avez-vous __traduit__ la page?*
	Have you translated/did you translate the page?
Voir:	*J'ai __vu__ mes amis.*
	I saw/have seen/did see my friends.
Vouloir:	*Elles ont __voulu__ attendre.*
	They wanted/did want to wait.

NOTE: Only the infinitives of irregular past participles are given in brackets in the examples in French in the appropriate chapters. (This means that irregular past participles of a few common verbs will be given a good numerous times. Repetition is the key to learning vocabulary.)

Helping you learn

Progress questions

1. What are the four different ways of saying that you have done something in the past in English which are discussed in this chapter?
2. How many rules are there governing formation of the past participle?
3. What are these rules?

Discussion points

1. Discuss rules for forming past participles in French with fellow students and anyone else interested in the subject.
2. Compare with English rules.

Practical assignment

Translate some of the English and some of the French examples.

> *Study tips*
> Read French as often as possible, if not every day.

Formation of the Perfect Tense with 'Avoir'

One-minute overview

This chapter looks at verbs that form the perfect tense using *avoir*. The appropriate examples in English given in Chapter One appear here in French and a few further examples have been added.

The sheer length of the list of examples is a good way of emphasising that there are up to four ways in English to say the same or nearly the same thing, but only one way of expressing all four in French.

Only verbs with irregular past participles are given in brackets from now on. This means that a few common and often very useful verbs such as *avoir* will be given a number of times: repetition is invaluable for learning a foreign language.

Examples are organised into separate lists; each list corresponds to the explanations of when to use the perfect tense provided in Chapter One. There is also a list containing additional examples.

> ➤ All transitive verbs (i.e. those that can take a direct object) and most intransitive verbs use *avoir* in compound tenses:

J'ai vu (voir) mon ami.
I saw my friend. I have seen my friend. I did see my friend.

Vous avez fini le travail.
You finished the work. You have finished the work. You did finish the work.

Il a téléphoné.
He phoned. He has phoned. He did phone.

On a parlé.
We spoke. We have spoken. We did speak.

Vous avez mangé au restaurant?
You ate out? Have you eaten out? Did you eat out?

J'ai lu (lire) ce livre deux fois.
I read this book twice. I have read this book twice. I did read this book twice.

Elle a eu (avoir) un rhume.
She had a cold. She has had a cold. She did have a cold.

J'ai passé mon permis de conduire en 1988.
I took my driving test in 1988. I have taken my driving test in 1988. I did take my driving test in 1988.

Son chat a regardé les oiseaux.
His cat watched the birds. His cat has been watching the birds. His cat did watch the birds.

Il y a eu (avoir) du bruit dehors.
There was some noise outside. There has been some noise outside.

Les lettres ont aidé ma mère.
The letters helped my mother. They have helped my mother. They did help my mother.

Le temps a changé.
The weather changed. The weather has changed. The weather did change.

Votre ami a envoyé des cadeaux?
Your friend sent presents? Has your friend sent presents? Did your friend send presents?

Le film a commencé en retard.
The film started late. The film has started late. The film did start late.

Ça a été (être) une longue semaine.
It was a long week. It has been a long week.

J'ai failli tomber.
I nearly fell. I did nearly fall.

Les prix ont baissé.
Prices dropped. Prices have dropped. Prices did drop.

Elle a battu tous les records.
She beat all records. She has beaten all records. She did beat all records.

Il a brisé mon coeur.
He broke my heart. He has broken my heart. He did break my heart.

Le chat a chassé l'écureuil.
The cat chased the squirrel. The cat has chased the squirrel. The cat did chase the squirrel.

Il a neigé.
It snowed. It has snowed. It has been snowing. It did snow.

Il a fallu (falloir) payer en euros.
It was necessary to pay in euros.

Elle a déjeuné, et elle a lu (lire) le journal.
She had lunch and read the newspaper.

Elles ont joué aux échecs.
They played chess.

J'ai dormi jusqu'à huit heures ce matin.
I slept until eight this morning.

Il a mangé des escargots, et il a été (être) si malade le lendemain qu'il a appelé le docteur.
He ate some snails and was so sick the next day that he called the doctor.

Il a demandé un café, puis il a téléphoné.
He asked for a coffee, and made a phone call.

J'ai pris (prendre) mon petit-déjeuner, puis j'ai quitté la maison.
I had breakfast, and left the house.

Le train a ralenti.
The train slowed down.

Il a fait (faire) froid ici.
It has been cold here.

* * *

Nous avons eu (avoir) froid toute la nuit.
We were/have been cold all night.

Ils ont habité à Marseille de 1969 à 2000.
They lived/did live in Marseilles from 1969 to 2000.

Il a attendu vingt minutes.
He waited/has waited/did wait twenty minutes.

Elles ont regardé la télévision de deux heures à cinq heures.
They watched/have watched/did watch television from two to five.

Il a plu (pleuvoir) toute la semaine.
It rained/has rained/did rain all week.

Ils ont chanté entre huit heures et dix heures.
They sang/did sing between eight and ten o'clock.

J'ai écrit (écrire) des lettres à mon ami anglais pendant dix ans.
I wrote/did write letters to my English friend for ten years.

Il a vécu (vivre) chez vous pendant combien d'années?
He lived with you for how many years?

Le chien a été (être) malade tout le week-end.
The dog was ill the whole weekend.

Ils ont défendu leur fils pendant longtemps.
They defended/did defend their son for a long time.

On a cuisiné tout le matin.
We cooked/have been cooking/did cook all morning.

La population a diminué au fil des années.
The population decreased/has decreased/did decrease over the years.

Cela a causé de la gêne pendant le reste du week-end.
It caused/has caused/did cause embarrassment for the rest of the weekend.

Il y a eu (avoir) beaucoup de bruit pendant au moins une heure.
There was a lot of noise for at least one hour.

Le week-end a été (être) barbant.
The weekend was/has been boring.

Il a plu (pleuvoir) tout le jour hier.
It rained all day yesterday.

Tu as révisé ce matin?
Have you been revising this morning?

* * *

Ça a été (être) une année triste.
It was/has been a sad year.

Tu as passé un bon après-midi?
Did you have a good afternoon?

Cela a été (être) des vacances onéreuses.
It was/has been an expensive holiday.

Elles ont passé un moment très heureux.
They had/have had a very happy time.

Elle a été (être) chanteuse.
She was/has been a singer.

Il a été (être) marié.
He was/has been married.

La fête a été (être) super?
Was the party/has the party been lovely?

Mon mari a apprécié son enfance.
My husband enjoyed his childhood.

Ils ont vraiment travaillé dur.
They have been working really hard.

J'ai regardé de vieilles photos.
I have been looking at old photographs.

On a aidé nos meilleurs amis à déménager.
We have been helping our best friends move house.

Il a lu (lire) le journal.
He has been reading the newspaper.

Elles ont parlé à leurs cousins.
They have been talking to their cousins.

Elle a perdu du poids pendant sa maladie.
She lost/has lost/did lose weight during her illness.

Ça a été (être) une expérience inoubliable.
It was/has been an unforgettable experience.

J'ai apprécié ce dernier cours.
I enjoyed/have enjoyed/did enjoy this last lesson.

* * *

J'ai mangé un curry plusieurs fois dans ce restaurant.
I had/have had curry several times in that restaurant.

Tu as passé ton permis de conduire trois fois?
Did you take your driving test three times?

On a écrit (écrire) plusieurs fois en décembre.
We wrote several times in December.

Ils ont joué ensemble tous les jours la semaine dernière.
They played together every day last week.

Elles ont téléphoné combien de fois aujourd'hui?
How many times did they ring today?

Mes parents ont pensé à nous tous les soirs le mois passé.
My parents thought about us every night last month.

Vous avez été (être) en retard combien de fois la semaine dernière?
How many times were you late last week?

J'ai vu (voir) le film deux fois et j'ai pleuré chaque fois.
I saw the film twice and cried each time.

J'ai remué la sauce à intervalles réguliers pendant une heure.
I stirred the sauce regularly for an hour.

Nous avons compté les billets au moins trois fois.
We counted the tickets at least three times.

Il a profité de chaque week-end pour refaire la cuisine.
He made the most of each weekend to redecorate the kitchen.

Elle a renversé son verre tous les soirs.
She spilled her glass each night.

* * *

Tout à coup j'ai été (être) inquiète.
Suddenly I was worried.

Vous avez eu (avoir) tort de crier.
You were wrong to shout.

Elle a été (être) très en colère.
She was very cross.

Il a été (être) gêné quand elle a dit (dire) ça.
He was embarrassed when she said that.

Nous avons été (être) déçus d'apprendre la nouvelle.
We were disappointed to hear the news.

Ils ont eu (avoir) l'air triste.
They looked sad.

J'ai dû (devoir) parler à mon patron tout de suite.
I needed to talk to my boss immediately.

Tu as eu (avoir) une surprise?
Have you had/did you have a surprise?

Vous avez eu (avoir) honte de vos résultats?
Were you ashamed of your results?

J'ai été (être) très émue lorsque j'ai vu (voir) la maison.
I was very moved when I saw the house.

Mon fils a eu (avoir) raison de partir.
My son was right to leave.

Il a eu (avoir) peur.
He got scared.

Elle a voulu (vouloir) tout quitter.
She wanted to leave everything.

On a espéré jusqu'au bout.
We hoped to the end.

Elles ont souhaité voir elles-mêmes.
They wanted to see for themselves.

J'ai été (être) stupéfait.
I was staggered.

Les enfants ont été (être) assez étonnés.
The children were quite surprised.

Les chiens ont été (être) contents de me voir.
The dogs were pleased to see me.

Cela a été (être) insupportable.
It was unbearable.

* * *

Subitement à neuf heures, j'ai eu (avoir) sommeil.
I was unexpectedly sleepy at nine.

Il a été (être) bête de croire son histoire.
He was stupid to believe his story.

Tout à coup il a eu (avoir) froid.
All of a sudden he was/got cold.

Après cinq heures les enfants ont eu (avoir) faim.
After five, children were/got hungry.

Les animaux ont eu (avoir) trop chaud cet été.
The animals got too hot this summer.

Ils ont eu (avoir) beaucoup de chance.
They were very lucky.

Il y a eu (avoir) du brouillard d'un seul coup.
All at once it got foggy.

C'est alors qu'il y a eu (avoir) un problème.
Then there was a problem.

Alors, il nous a fallu (falloir) partir.
So, we had to go.

Il y a eu (avoir) beaucoup de questions.
There were many questions.

Soudain il y a eu (avoir) un cri.
Suddenly there was a scream.

Après ça, la rue a été (être) silencieuse.
After that the street was quiet.

Vous avez eu (avoir) trop confiance en lui.
You trusted him too much.

J'ai été (être) étonnée de les voir là.
I was surprised to see them there.

Il a fallu prendre une décision.
We had to decide.

Il est évident qu'il y a eu (avoir) un malentendu.
There clearly was a misunderstanding.

Elle a eu (avoir) trente ans samedi dernier.
She was thirty last Saturday.

C'est là que j'ai eu (avoir) l'idée.
That's when I had the idea.

* * *

La vendeuse a été (être) serviable hier.
The shop assistant was helpful yesterday.

Quand j'ai eu (avoir) vingt ans (j'ai décidé d'acheter une voiture).
When I was (turned) twenty (I decided to buy a car).

On a voulu (vouloir) faire une différence.
We wanted to make a difference.

C'est ce qu'elle a pensé.
That's what she thought.

Elle a eu (avoir) envie d'aller au cinéma.
She fancied going to the cinema.

Tu as eu (avoir) l'air content (quand le téléphone a sonné).
You looked pleased (when the phone rang).

Mon père est le seul qui a compris (comprendre) mon frère.
Only my father understood my brother.

Il a eu (avoir) l'air contrarié.
He looked upset.

Cela a été (être) impossible.
It was impossible.

J'ai voulu (vouloir) parler au professeur hier.
I wanted to speak to the teacher yesterday.

Ils ont pensé que ce serait mieux.
They thought that it would be better.

Ils ont voulu (vouloir) y assister.
They wanted to be there.

Ça a été (être) fatigant?
Was it tiring?

Nous avons pensé le contraire.
We thought the opposite.

Tu as eu (avoir) l'air effrayé.
You looked frightened.

* * *

Il a voulu (vouloir) changer la voiture.
He wanted to change the car.

Nous avons pu (pouvoir) le faire.
We were able to do it.

Mes frères ont été (être) fiers.
My brothers were proud.

Vous avez donné un bon conseil.
You have given/gave/did give good advice.

Le voyage a duré une heure.
The journey has lasted/lasted/did last one hour.

J'ai nettoyé le salon.
I have cleaned/have been cleaning/cleaned/did clean the lounge.

La police a poursuivi (poursuivre) la voiture jusqu'au village voisin.
The police have chased/chased/did chase the car to the next village.

Nous avons décidé de déménager.
We have decided/decided/did decide to move house.

Vous avez signé où?
Where have you signed/did you sign?

Elle a saisi l'occasion.
She has seized/seized/did seize the opportunity.

Le soleil a brillé tout le jour.
The sun has shined/has been shining/shone/did shine all day.

Qu'est-ce qu'il a touché?
What has he touched/did he touch?

Ils ont dormi sur la plage?
Have they slept/have they been sleeping/did they sleep on the beach?

La compagnie a licencié deux personnes.
The company has made/made/did make two people redundant.

J'ai conduit (conduire) comme une folle ce matin.
I have driven/ have been driving/drove/did drive dangerously this morning.

Vous avez glissé sur le verglas?
Have you slid/did you slide on the ice?

Le prix a changé.
The price has changed/changed/did change.

Deux adolescents ont saccagé l'ascenseur de l'immeuble.
Two teenagers have vandalised/vandalised/did vandalise the lift in the block of flats.

Ma mère a gagné à la loterie.
My mother has won/won/did win the lottery.

Est-ce qu'il a informé le docteur?
Has he informed/did he inform the doctor?

L'avion a décollé à quelle heure?
The plane has taken/took/did take off at what time?

Est-ce que l'eau a boulli?
Has the water boiled/did the water boil?

Nous ne savons pas qui a garni cette table.
We don't know who decorated/has decorated/did decorate this table.

Helping you learn

Progress questions

1. What is a transitive verb?
2. Do these verbs need *avoir* or *être* to form the perfect tense?

Discussion points

1. Discuss the difference between the four different ways of talking about the past in English with fellow students or any willing listener.
2. Discuss instances when there would be subtle differences in meaning between them.

Practical assignment

Translate some of the English and some of the French examples in Chapter Three.

Study tips

Listening to spoken French at every opportunity can only accelerate learning.

4

Formation of the Perfect Tense with 'Etre'

One-minute overview

This chapter deals with verbs that form the perfect tense using *être*. Although the basic formation of the past participles is the same for all verbs in the perfect tense, there is a difference to take into account.

The translation of all the appropriate examples given in English in Chapter One, as well as a few additional examples, illustrate the formation of the perfect tense for verbs that use *être*.

■ A number of verbs do not form the perfect tense with 'avoir' but with 'être' (still in the present tense and with the appropriate past participle). The main ones that are useful in everyday conversation are:

Aller
Arriver
Descendre
Devenir
Entrer
Monter
Mourir
Naître
Partir
Passer
Rester
Retourner
Sortir
Tomber
Venir

■ As well as advising students to learn this by heart, suggested explanations of when to use 'être' and 'avoir,' and ways in which to describe the verbs include:

➢ With a few/a dozen or so/a small group of/a few very common verbs.

➢ Most of these verbs are verbs of motion: they express a general idea of movement, of coming and going. (Note that *être* is <u>not</u> used with <u>all</u> verbs of motion, far from it. 'to run,' 'to jump,' 'to dance' 'to walk,' for example, form the perfect tense using *avoir*, not *être*.)

➢ Some of these verbs express a change of state (*devenir, mourir, naître,* and perhaps *rester*).

➢ Ten of the verbs can be remembered in five pairs which are opposite in meaning (*aller-venir, arriver-partir, entrer-sortir, monter-descendre* and *naître-mourir*).

➢ With verbs whose common feature is either that they cannot take a direct object (i.e. intransitive verbs) or that they don't need a direct object to complete their meaning.

NOTE: All verbs derived from the verbs listed above fall into the same category (for example: *tomber*, to fall, and *retomber*, to fall again, *venir*, to come, and *revenir*, to come back, *entrer*, to go in, and *rentrer*, to get in/get back home).

■ One very important difference, especially as regards written French, between the group of verbs that use 'être' and those which take 'avoir' is that with 'être' the past participle is treated like an adjective, agreeing with the subject (the doer of the action) in gender (masculine or feminine) and number (singular or plural), as follows:

Claude est sorti (**m.s.**)
Antoine est sorti (**m.s.**)

Antoine et Claude sont sorti<u>s</u> (**m.p.**)
Valérie est sorti<u>e</u> (**f.s.**)
Stéphanie est sorti<u>e</u> (**f.s.**)
Valérie et Stéphanie sont sort<u>ies</u> (**f.p.**)
Antoine et Stéphanie sont sorti<u>s</u> (**mixed**)
Valérie et Claude sont sorti<u>s</u> (**mixed**)

NOTE: The added 's' that indiactes the plural is only pronounced when a liaison between two words may be made, which is not the case after a past participle. The feminine agreement affects the pronunciation of a past participle only when it ends with a consonant, therefore of the *être* verbs listed above, this would only apply to *mourir*: 'mort' and 'morts' in 'il est mort,' and in 'ils sont morts' have the same pronunciation, whereas the past participle in the feminine forms is pronounced as two syllables, 'elle est morte' and 'elles sont mortes.'

Elle est tombée.
She fell. She has fallen. She did fall.

Ils sont allés à Paris?
They went to Paris? Have they gone to Paris? Did they go to Paris?

Les livres sont tombés par terre.
The books fell on the floor. They have fallen on the floor. They did fall on the floor.

Son chien est mort (mourir)?
Her dog died? Has her dog died? Did her dog die?

La voiture est tombée en panne?
The car broke down? Has it broken down? Did it break down?

Êtes-vous né/nés/née/nées (naître) en provence?
Were you born in Provence?

Elles sont devenues (devenir) pauvres.
They became poor. They have become poor. They did become poor.

Elle est venue (venir).
She came. She has come. She did come.

Ils sont allés au restaurant hier soir, et ils sont rentrés à onze heures.
They went/did go to a restaurant last night, and came/did come home at eleven.

Il est arrivé.
He arrived. He has arrived. He did arrive.

Je suis descendu/descendue.
I went down. I have gone down. I did go down.

Les chiot sont nés (naître) ce matin, mais deux sont morts (mourir) une heure après.
The puppies were born this morning, but two died an hour later.

Le train est apparu (apparaître) dans le brouillard.
The train appeared/has appeared/did appear in the fog.

* * *

Je suis resté/restée au lit deux jours.
I stayed/did stay in bed for two days.

Vous êtes resté/restée/restés/restées longtemps?
You stayed/did you stay a long time?

Elle est venue (venir) avec nous plusieurs fois pendant l'été.
She came with us several times in the summer.

Je suis allé/allée en France tous les ans avant mon mariage.
I went to France every year before my marriage.

Elle est allée à l'hôpital toutes les semaines pendant trois mois.
She went to the hospital every week for three months.

C'est arrivé trois fois.
It happened three times. It has happened three times. It did happen three times.

Après ça tout le monde est parti.
After that everyone left.

* * *

Je suis venu/venue (venir)
I came/have come/did come.

Tu es arrivé/arrivée à quelle heure?
At what time did you arrive?

Ils sont entrés ensemble.
They went in/have gone in/did go in together.

Quand est-ce que vous êtes descendu/descendue/descendus/descendues?
When did you go down?

Pourquoi est-ce qu'il est venu (venir)?
Why did/has he come?

Elles sont arrivées à trois heures.
They arrived/did arrive at three.

Claude est né (naître) en France.
Claude was born in France.

Un grand malheur est survenu (survenir) à cette famille.
Something absolutely dreadful happened/has happened/did happen to this family.

Ils sont intervenus (intervenir) à temps.
They intervened/have intervened/did intervene in time.

Leur lettre est parvenue (parvenir) au maire ce matin.
Their letter reached/has reached/did reach the mayor this morning.

L'annonce est apparue (apparaître) dans le magazine la semaine passée.
The advert appeared/has appeared/did appear in the magazine last week.

Stéphanie est montée au troisième étage.
Stéphanie went up/has gone up/did go up to the third floor.

Il est intervenu (intervenir) quand exactement?
When exactly did he intervene?

Elles sont parvenues (parvenir) à leur but?
Have they succeeded/did they succeed in their quest?

Une complication est survenue (survenir) deux jours plus tard.
Two days later, a complication arose.

Valérie et Bernard sont partis mardi.
Bernard and Valérie left/did leave on Tuesday.

Il est accouru (accourir) vers moi pour m'accueillir.
He rushed up/has rushed up/did rush up to welcome me.

Ils sont revenus (revenir) plusieurs fois.
They came back/did come back several times.

Nous sommes devenus (devenir) riches.
We became/did become rich.

Les filles sont sorties à huit heures.
The girls went out/did go out at eight.

C'est devenu (devenir) trop compliqué.
It became/got too complicated.

Ils sont venus (venir) toutes les semaines en novembre.
They came/did come every week in November.

*However, some of the verbs in the list of verbs that take 'être'
in the perfect tense may in fact also be conjugated with 'avoir,'
when they can take an object and have slightly different
meanings:*

J'ai monté le livre.
I took/have taken/did take the book upstairs.

Tu as descendu la chaise?
Have you brought/did you bring the chair down?

Elle a rentré le linge.
She got/has got/did get the washing in.

Il a passé le journal à son père.
He passed/has passed/did pass the newspaper to his father.

On a sorti les photos du mariage.
We got/did get the wedding photographs out.

Nous avons retourné les compliments.
We returned/have returned/did return the compliments.

Il a monté les valises au deuxième étage.
He took/has taken/did take the suitcases up to the second floor.

Elles ont descendu les sacs.
They took/have taken/did take the bags down.

Ils ont rentré les plantes.
They brought/have brought/did bring the plants indoors.

J'ai monté le bébé.
I took/have taken/did take the baby upstairs.

Tu as descendu les boîtes?
Have you taken/did you take the boxes downstairs?

Elle a rentré la voiture au garage.
She put/has put/did put the car in the garage.

Il a passé la moutarde à sa fille.
He passed/has passed/did pass the mustard to his daughter.

On a sorti nos plus jolies tasses.
We took/have taken/did take out our prettiest cups.

Nous avons retourné les livres à la bibliothèque.
We returned/have returned/did return the books to the library.

Vous avez passé l'hôtel de ville?
Have you gone/did you go past the town hall?

Elles ont descendu les robes.
They took/have taken/did take the dresses downstairs.

J'ai sorti la poubelle trop tard.
I took/have taken/did take the dustbin out too late.

Ils ont passé le pont.
They went/have gone/did go past the bridge.

Il a monté le courrier dans la chambre.
He took/has taken/did take the post upstairs.

Helping you learn

Progress questions

1. Which are the main verbs used in conversation that form the perfect tense with *être*?
2. How can these verbs be described?
3. How does using *être* instead of *avoir* affect the past participle?

Discussion points

Discuss the answers to the questions above with others.

Practical assignment

1. Translate some of the French or English examples in this chapter.
2. Check your answers.

Study tips
Mix both languages: Replace English with the French you know when you are thinking.

5

Formation of the Perfect Tense with Reflexive Verbs

All verbs that are <u>reflexive</u> in form (i.e. the action refers back to the subject) also form the perfect tense using *être*. There are more reflexive verbs in French than there are in English.

There are a few rules regarding the agreement of the past participle with reflexive verbs; these rules differ from those discussed in the previous chapter.

■ With reflexive verbs, the subject and reflexive pronouns refer to the same person or thing. The reflexive pronoun of a reflexive verb is <u>almost</u> always its direct object.

■ Reflexive verbs could be described as hybrid; although they form the perfect with the verb *être*, the agreement of the past participle with the direct object (masculine, feminine, singular or plural) actually follows the rules that apply to *avoir* verbs (see Chapter Eleven). With reflexive verbs, the reflexive pronoun is not only the same person or thing as the subject, it is often also the direct object:

Je me suis coupé (**m.s.**)
Il s'est coupé (**m.s.**)
Je me suis coupée (**f.s.**)
Elle s'est coupée (**f.s.**)
Nous nous sommes coupés (**m.p. or mixed**)
Nous nous sommes coupées (**f.p.**)
Ils se sont coupés (**m.p. or mixed**)
Elles se sont coupées (**f.p.**)

> ➤ When the last letter of a past participle is a consonant and an 'e' is added for the feminine form, pronunciation is slightly affected and there is one additional syllable:

Vous vous êtes plaint? (**m.s.**)
Vous vous êtes plaints? (**m.p.**)
Vous vous êtes plaints? (**mixed**)
Vous vous êtes plainte? (**f.s.**)
Vous vous êtes plaintes? (**f.p.**)

Je me suis couché/couchée à onze heures, et je me suis levé/levée vers neuf heures.
I went to bed at eleven and I got up at about nine.

Je me suis réveillé/réveillée, je me suis levé/levée, je me suis lavé/lavée et je me suis habillé/habillée.
I woke up, got up, washed and dressed.

Elle s'est ennuyée chez sa tante.
She was bored at her aunt's.

Ils se sont plaints/Elles se sont plaintes (se plaindre).
They complained/have complained/did complain.

Est-ce que tu t'es excusé/excusée?
Have you apologised? Did you apologise?

Il s'est assis (s'asseoir).
He sat down/has sat down/did sit down.

Le train s'est arrêté.
The train stopped/has stopped/did stop.

Ils se sont baladés au bord de la mer.
They strolled/have strolled/did stroll/have been strolling by the sea.

Vous vous êtes amusé/amusée/amusés/amusées cet après-midi?
Have you enjoyed/did you enjoy yourself/yourselves this afternoon?

Les oiseaux se sont égosillés pendant au moins une heure.
The birds sang at the top of their voices for at least one hour.

Est-ce qu'elles se sont reconnues (se reconnaître)?
Have they recognised/did they recognise each other?

Les travaux se sont effectués en trois jours.
The work was/has been carried out in three days.

Je me suis amusé/amusée à la fête.
I had/have had a lot of fun at the party.

Il s'est aperçu (s'apercevoir) de l'erreur?
Has he noticed/did he notice the mistake?

Elle s'est approchée de nous.
She moved/has moved/did move towards us.

Le bus s'est arrêté devant la gare.
The bus stopped/has stopped/did stop outside the station.

Ils se sont assis ici (s'asseoir).
They sat down/have sat down/did sit down here.

Je me suis brûlé/brûlée.
I burnt/have burnt/did burn myself.

Tu t'es coiffé/coiffée?
Have you combed/did you comb your hair?

L'eau s'est évaporée.
The water evaporated/has evaporated/did evaporate.

Vous vous êtes débrouillé/débrouillée/débrouillés/débrouillées?
Have you managed/did you manage?

Est-ce qu'ils se sont dépêchés?
Have they been hurrying up/did they hurry up?

Nous nous sommes disputés/disputées.
We argued/have argued/have been arguing/did argue.

Elle s'est mariée en Normandie.
She got married in Normandy.

Ils se sont penchés ensemble.
They bent forward/did bend forward together.

Ils se sont promenés au bord du lac.
They had/have had/did have a walk by the lake.

Vous vous êtes compris/comprises (comprendre) à la fin?
Did you understand one another in the end?

Elle s'est assise (s'asseoir) où?
Where has she sat down/did she sit down?

Tu t'es reposé/reposée tout le jour?
Have you rested/did you rest the whole day?

Je me suis réveillé/réveillée tard aujourd'hui.
I woke up/have woken up/did wake up late today.

Les jeunes se sont sauvés après l'accident.
The youths ran away/did run away after the accident.

Ils se sont souvenus (se souvenir) de ça.
They remembered/have remembered/did remember that.

Nous nous sommes trompés/trompées.
We made/have made/did make a mistake.

Les enfants se sont éclatés à la plage.
The children had a ball on the beach.

Ils se sont regardés.
They looked/have looked/did look at each other.

Le bébé s'est endormi dans mes bras.
The baby fell/has fallen/did fall asleep in my arms.

Elles se sont occupées tout le matin.
They busied/did busy themselves the whole morning.

Tu t'es bien restauré/restaurée?
Have you had/did you have enough food and drink?

Je me suis souvenu/souvenue (se souvenir) de l'hôtel.
I remembered/have remembered/did remember the hotel.

Vous vous êtes trompé/trompée/trompés/trompées.
You made/have made/did make a mistake.

Nous nous sommes revus/revues le lendemain (se revoir).
We saw/did see each other again the next day.

La fête s'est achevée avec des feux d'artifice.
The party ended with fireworks.

Elle s'est appuyée sur lui.
She leant on him.

Nous nous sommes chargés de tout ça nous-mêmes.
We took care of all that ourselves.

Les gosses se sont balancés tout l'après-midi.
The kids were on the swing all afternoon.

Il s'est rappelé trop tard.
He remembered too late.

Elles se sont relevées ensemble.
They stood up together.

■ When, as in English, the reflexive pronoun is the indirect object (governed by a **preposition** which, depending on the construction of the sentence, can be omitted in English), there is no agreement of the past participle:

Ils/elles se sont parlé.
They spoke/have spoken/did speak **to each other**.

Nous nous sommes écrit (écrire) pendant six mois.
We wrote/did write **to each other** for six months.

Est-ce que vous vous êtes donné des cadeaux?
Have you given/did you give presents **to one another**?

Vous vous êtes prêté combien de vidéos?
How many videos did you lend **(to) one another**?

Vous vous êtes parlé au téléphone?
Did you speak **to one another** on the phone?

Ils/elles se sont menti.
They lied **to** each other:

> ■ Another difficulty is that some verbs require a
> preposition in French but not in English, for example,
> in France we telephone **to** people (*téléphoner* **à**), we
> ask **to** people (*demander* **à**), we forbid **to** people
> (*interdire à*) and we tell **to** people (*dire à*):

Est-ce que vous vous êtes téléphoné tous les jours?
Did you phone/have you phoned each other every day?

Valérie et Stéphanie se sont téléphoné à Noël.
Valérie and Stéphanie phoned each other at Christmas.

Elle s'est demandé la même chose.
She asked herself (wondered)/has asked herself/did ask
herself the same thing.

C'est ce que nous nous sommes demandé.
That is what we wondered.

Elles se sont interdit de fumer dans l'appartement.
They forbade themselves to smoke in the flat.

C'est ce que nous nous sommes dit.
That is what we told ourselves.

> ■ On the other hand, and finally, a reflexive verb can
> sometimes also have a direct object that is not the
> reflexive pronoun, when the reflexive pronoun again
> is an indirect object (especially by virtue of the rule
> that in French a verb cannot have two direct objects):

Elle *s'est lavée.*
She washed/has washed/did wash herself.

but

*Elle s'est lavé **les mains**.*
She washed/has washed/did wash her hands.

(literally: She washed to herself the hands).

*__Elise et Elodie__ se sont lav**ées**.*
Elise and Elodie washed/have washed/did wash (themselves).

but

__Roxanne et Caroline__ se sont lavé __la tête__.
Roxanne and Caroline have washed their hair.

*__Caroline__ s'est coup**ée**.*
Caroline has cut herself.

but

Caroline s'est coupé __deux doigts__.
Caroline cut/has cut/did cut two fingers.

*__Les biscuits__ se sont cass**és** pendant le voyage.*
The biscuits broke during the journey.

but

Valérie et Stéphanie se sont cassé __la jambe__ toutes les deux.
Both Valérie and Stéphanie broke/have broken/did break their legs.

Helping you learn

Progress questions

1. What is a reflexive verb?
2. Which auxiliary verb is used with these verbs to form the perfect tense?
3. What are the different rules that govern agreement of the past participles?

Discussion points

If there is only one way in French to translate up to four ways of expressing what you or others did, the extra rules to remember for forming the perfect tense 'compensate'!

Practical assignment

1. Translate some of the French and English examples in the different sections of this chapter.
2. Check your answers.

> **Study tips**
> Use French instead of English when writing short messages (emails, mobile phone texts) to fellow students and anyone with your level of French, or when writing lists of things to do or shopping lists.

6

Exceptions

One-minute overview

As mentioned before, the French perfect tense is used in ordinary, everyday conversations, in informal accounts and in informal letters.

This chapter deals with instances when the past tense is used in English, but the present tense is used in French. It also suggests how tenses can be manipulated in order to achieve a certain style. The lists of examples that follow illustrate the different explanations.

■ As mentioned earlier there are two key structures that require the perfect tense in English but not in French. Instead, they use the present tense:

➤ DEPUIS key structure (when an action which was started in the past is <u>not yet</u> <u>completed</u>):

We have worked/have been working in the garden for twenty minutes.

They have shared/have been sharing a bedroom for two months.

How long have you been here?

Someone has been knocking at the door for five minutes.

It has been raining for three days.

I have been worrying for three hours/since three o'clock.

They have lived/have been living in France since 1992.

He has been learning French for several months now.

She has had a temperature since Monday.

We have been cold since last night.

> ➤ VENIR DE key structure (to have just done something):

I have just seen the postman.

You have just missed your friend.

She has just finished.

He has just fallen.

We have just asked.

Have you just had a shower?

They have just asked.

Something has just creaked.

I have just pumped the tyres.

We have just checked.

Note: Full explanations of these key structures are given in Chapter Thirteen, together with the translations of the examples above and a few further examples.

■ As with English, a news story in the form of an article (newspaper headlines in particular) or a radio or television story can be mostly recounted in the present tense. The present tense can also be used in certain types of written or oral narrations aimed at the general public, such as historical descriptions. As in English, the use of the present tense in French in place of a past tense achieves a particular style of expression, giving a sense of immediacy to an event or sequence of events:

Un père de quatre enfants tue sa femme dans un village provençal.
A father of four kills his wife in a village in Provence.

Une jeune femme accouche au cinéma.
A young woman has a baby in the cinema.

Le politicien s'explique longuement devant un public cynique.
The politician takes ages to explain himself to a cynical public.

L' avion s'écrase quelques minutes avant l'heure d'arrivée.
A plane crashes a few minutes before it was due to land.

L'acteur remporte son troisième prix en deux ans.
The actor wins his third prize in two years.

Un alcoolique se jette dans la rivière.
An alcoholic throws himself into the river.

Le lendemain, le jeune homme se procure la drogue.
The next day the youth gets hold of the drug.

La victime hurle, et l'adolescent tire.
As the victim screams, the teenager shoots.

■ Similarly, and confusingly, it is also possible to see the imperfect tense (see Chapter Seven) used in place of the perfect tense, again for stylistic reasons:

At eleven, the Queen arrived at the cathedral for her mother's funeral.

In 1995, the famous couple divorced.

On the third of May 1965, the singer was born.

At eight, the plane landed as expected.

The next day, the press announced the President's resignation.

At dawn, the boat capsized.

That year, he was to finish his law degree.

That morning, the company announced bankruptcy.

The following year, the couple adopted a child.

At around 2 a.m. the neighbours heard screams.

NOTE: In French, the events or actions in these instances are usually introduced by <u>when</u> they happened.

■ The past historic (le passé simple – see Chapter Fourteen) replaces the perfect tense in certain written works, formal literary stories, paragraphs or articles and in novels. People who can handle the perfect and imperfect tenses, should and would probably recognise and understand verbs in the past historic, especially in context. It is extremely unlikely that you would hear this 'narrative tense par excellence' used in everyday conversation.

Helping you learn

Progress questions

1. What are the two key structures that require the perfect tense in English but the present tense in French?
2. In what other instances can the perfect tense be replaced by other tenses?

Discussion points

1. Discuss answers above.
2. Discuss similarities and differences between the two languages with fellow students and anyone else interested in the subject.

Practical assignment

Remember this chapter when next reading English as well as French newspapers or magazines.

Study tips

1. Never miss an opportunity to speak French, even if only one word or a few words mixed with English.
2. Little and often works well.

7

When to use the Imperfect Tense

One-minute overview

As in English everyday speech, the imperfect tense is usually found in combination with the perfect tense. The <u>main</u> differences between the perfect tense and the imperfect tense is that whereas the perfect means a finished action or a situation that occurred at a precise moment in the past, the imperfect is used with unfinished, continuous actions or for actions that were habitual, with unknown or vague start and finish times and without precise limits in time. It is also the tense used when discussing situations that existed already, including descriptions of things and people.

Rule one of the imperfect tense can be explained in several ways:

■ To describe recurring actions or situations that were habitual, customary, routine, repeated, regular, frequent, that took place an indefinite number of times and mostly without precise times;

■ To convey the underlying idea of 'used to do' or 'would do' something, and in certain contexts 'kept doing' something;

■ In fact, whenever 'used/would do' could be inserted in order to clarify the exact meaning of a verb in the English simple past tense, the imperfect tense is required in French.

Every morning he got up/he used to get up/he would get up at exactly 6 o'clock.

Sometimes my husband used to/would watch the game shows with me.

Years ago, my grandmother used to buy all her presents at Harrods.

We used to encourage our children to learn more French every time we went to France.

My sons kept insisting on that.

I used to give sweets to my friend's children.

She would always give homeless men or women a cigarette or a coin.

You always used to act before thinking.

They used to go out every Saturday.

They kept asking the same question every ten minutes.

He used to give lily of the valley to all his sisters on the first of May.

They used to go to the theatre a lot before they had the children.

They kept sending emails.

When the dogs were puppies, they would bite our slippers.

Grandad used to repair our bikes.

People used to organise street parties.

We always forgot to send them a card.

You insulted my sister regularly.

She always came home tired.

Their father used to do weight lifting.

Rule two can also be described in a number of ways:

- To describe what the situation, the circumstances, the state of things, were like in the past;
- To say how people or things looked or seemed in the past,
- or what was true of them;
- To express general past feelings.

I couldn't afford to buy a computer then.

When we lived in Berkshire, my sister worked in a bank.

When I was a teenager, I wanted six children.

He was the best dentist in the area.

We were cold in that old tent.

The children were asleep.

Was the sun shining?

It was their turn to drive.

Prices were high that year.

I always believed my friend in those days.

The weather was poor yesterday.

Why were you hungry?

They had a set idea.

She was their favourite daughter.

It was hot in that shop.

She had a headache.

He had blond hair when he was young.

The teacher was wearing a black suit, and looked very pleased with himself.

They were German.

We were worried about you when you went rock climbing.

NOTE: Rule two seems to apply especially to the verbs *avoir*, *être*, *pouvoir* and *devoir*.

There are various ways to describe rule three as follows:

■ For general descriptions in the past.
■ To set the scene in a story.
■ To give the background in certain types of narrative.
■ To add descriptive detail to stories in the past.

The house was yellow.

The castle was impressive.

There were lots of photographs in the lounge.

It was already midnight.

The church was on a hill.

The fence was broken.

Their first car was green.

The campsite had two stars.

My friend's house was very old.

There were at least one hundred people at the meeting.

Our kitchen was small.

It was cloudy.

There often were traffic jams at peak times.

There used to be an apple tree here.

It was dark and cold.

All the shutters on the houses were closed.

The street was deserted.

There used to be a bidet in their bathroom.

They used to be my neighbours.

It was me.

NOTE 1: This last rule means that in speech about the past, *était* (was), especially in '*c'était*' (it/that/this was), is used frequently in descriptions, and for identification and naming purposes (to say who or what he/she/it was/used to be, or who or what they were/used to be):

It was sad.
It was excellent.
It was very strange.

It was horrible.
It was ridiculous.
It was difficult.

He was a dentist.
She was a singer.
She was his wife.
He was the priest.
He was an idiot.
They were his/her friends.

It was an important day.
It was a mistake.
It was a Tuesday.
It was a small boat.
It was a problem.
It was a miracle.

NOTE 2: Another expression in the imperfect tense
commonly employed in past descriptions is '*il y avait*'
('there was/were,' or 'there used to be'):

There were lots of people in town yesterday.
There was a lovely view from the hotel.
There were live rabbits at the market.
There were too many problems.
In my grandparents' house there was a cellar.
There was a good choice of books.

NOTE 3: However, when '*il y avait*' means 'there used to
be' with the emphasis on 'but not now, not anymore,' it is
usually preceded by '*avant*' (before):

There used to be a cinema in my street.

There used to be a large plane tree in front of the block of flats.

There used to be a fireplace in this room.

There used to be only one school in the village.

There used to be a factory near here.

There always used to be apple tart on Sundays.

Rule four can be explained in several different ways:

> ◼ Incomplete, unfinished, continuous actions or events in the past;
> ◼ Actions in the process of happening;
> ◼ Events in the process of taking place;
> ◼ To denote an action or process taking place at a particular point in time when something or someone was interrupted;
> ◼ To say what you or others were doing;
> ◼ To translate 'was' or 'were' + the present participle.

I was crossing the street (when I saw Roxanne).

They were still asleep at eleven!

He was working at eleven o'clock in the evening last Saturday.

He was reading (when you phoned).

The children were drinking lemonade.

He was finishing his meal.

They were watching a film at midnight.

I was leaving the house (when my mobile rang).

He was dressing in a hurry.

They were smoking (when I came in).

The snow was already melting.

We were travelling too fast.

She was listening to the radio.

They were leaving (when I arrived).

I was thinking.

What were you saying to my wife?

She was dreaming.

We were making the beds.

It was raining yesterday.

NOTE: 'Etre (in the imperfect) en train de' + infinitive is an alternative construction for rule four.

> ■ **Rule five:** 'if' clauses that introduce a condition or a supposition, what one <u>would do if</u> conditions were different, if conditions allowed it, plausible suppositions as well as unlikely ones (dreams) are followed by a verb in the imperfect tense then the second verb in the conditional tense:

If I won the lottery, I would buy a holiday home in France.

If they could, they would change a lot of things.

What would you say if we changed our minds?

Would you cry if I left?

We would be pleased if she came.

If he were to ask, we would accept.

They would probably understand if we explained the situation.

Would you do it if you were free?

They would come if they wanted to.

If I had the time I would travel more.

If I were you I would get divorced.

If I could I would do it.

If she lent her brother her bike, she would regret it.

If they had the money, they would buy a motorhome.

I would hate it if my daughter went to live abroad.

Would you mind if we parked here?

Would she rent a house if she went to live in London?

The dogs would hate it if we were to put them in kennels.

How would you manage if you were made redundant?

If we were upset we would say so.

> ➤ The same tense is used when simply expressing a wish or a supposition with the sense of 'if only...' when the possibilities are not only left unsaid, but are in all probablity only dreams:

If only I had the money...
If only you were here...
If only she could come...
If only it were possible...
If only it were true...
If only you were younger...

> **Exceptions**
> *As is the case in English, it is also sometimes possible for the verb that follows 'if' to be in the present tense, when both actions mentioned are in fact quite possible or probable. However, in this instance, the subsequent verb is also in the present in French:*

Si je gagne à la loterie, j'achète une résidence secondaire en France.
If I win the lottery, I 'll buy a holiday home in France.

Si tu pars je pleure.
If you go, I'll cry.

S'il demande, on accepte.
If he does ask, we'll accept.

S'ils viennent, elle part.
If they come, she'll leave.

Si tu fais ça je te parle plus.
If you do that, I won't talk to you any more.

S'il pleut on reste à la maison.
If it rains, we'll stay in.

> ■ Rule five: One way to make a suggestion or a supposition, such as 'How about doing this or that,' requires the imperfect tense in French preceded by 'and if':

What about going to the cinema/Shall we go to the cinema?

What if we refused?

What about eating out tonight?

What if I phoned tomorrow?

What if we tried/Shall we try?

What if it rains?

> ■ Rule six: In reported speech, also known as indirect speech, any verb that was in the present tense takes the imperfect tense:

We said that we were bored.

I said that I had three grandchildren.

I was asked whether I had time to come on Saturday.

We said that we must leave at six.

She told her parents that she was ill.

I said that I enjoyed playing chess.

They said that they were Irish.

Did you say that you knew my mother?

I told my boss that I had problems with my computer.

They said that they wanted to get involved.

We said that we were moving house in February.

He told my friend that he was married.

We said that we had two brothers working abroad.

They said that they must leave on Monday.

He asked the children whether they could speak French.

She said that she wanted to come again.

You mentioned that you could guarantee a date.

I said that I had a new mobile phone.

He asked if the car went well/was going well.

He informed the staff that everyone had to work overtime today.

> **Exception**
>
> *As is the case in English, in some cases, reported speech uses the <u>present</u> tense. This is the case when referring to something that is actually taking place here and now, perhaps when someone didn't hear what was said or is surprised at what they are hearing:*

Elle dit qu'il pleut.
She says that it is raining.

Il dit qu'il apprend à conduire.
He says that he is learning to drive.

Ils sont d'accord que c'est cher.
They agree that it is expensive.

Tu dis qu'ils ont huit chats?
Are you saying that they have eight cats?

Elles disent qu'elles aiment cette plage.
They say that they like this beach.

Elle dit qu'elle déteste le couscous.
She says that she hates couscous.

> ■ Rule seven: The imperfect tense can also be used in place of the perfect tense in news stories (not in everyday conversation) in order to achieve a particular effect: to emphasise an exceptional occurrence or

incident, or an action that, for a number of reasons, is out of the ordinary. The English equivalent is perhaps the construction 'somebody <u>was to do</u> something' with the meaning 'somebody <u>did</u> something':

At eleven, the Queen arrived at the cathedral for her mother's funeral.

In 1995, the famous couple divorced.

On the third of May 1965, the singer was born.

At eight, the plane landed as expected.

The next day, the press announced the President's resignation.

At dawn, the boat capsized.

That year, he was to finish his law degree.

That morning, the company announced bankruptcy.

Helping you learn

Progress questions

1. What are the rules governing when to use the imperfect tense?
2. What are the exceptions?
3. Check your answers.

Discussion points

1. Discuss rules governing the use of the imperfect tense with fellow students and anyone else interested in the subject.
2. Discuss exceptions.
3. Compare use of the tense with the English equivalent.

Practical assignment

1. Write a few English examples from each set of examples on small pieces of paper.
2. Mix the examples well and then sort them into rule groups.
3. Check your work.

Study tips

1. Read and re-read rules and appropriate examples until you have absorbed the rules.
2. Little and often works well.

Formation of the Imperfect Tense

Compared to the formation of the perfect tense, the formation of the imperfect tense (a 'simple tense,' i.e. one word) is very straight-forward. There is only one verb that doesn't follow the rule.

■ Imperfect endings are added to the verb stem, also known as the root. In order to get the verb stem, you take the present tense of the verb with '*nous*' (we), for example:

Nous sortons
Nous voyons
Nous devons
Nous fournissons
Nous nous couchons
Nous revenons
Nous demandons
Nous avons
Nous croyons
Nous descendons

■ Remove '*ons,*' the present tense ending for 'nous':

Nous sort__
Nous voy__
Nous dev__
Nous fourniss__
Nous nous couch__
Nous reven__
Nous demand__
Nous av__

Nous croy___
Nous descend___

■ The one exception to this rule is *être*:

The verb stem for 'to be' is: ét___

■ The endings to add to verb stems to form the imperfect tense are as follows:

Je:	___ais
Tu:	___ais
Il/Elle/On:	___ait
Nous:	___ions
Vous:	___iez
Ils/Elles:	___aient

NOTE: There are only three different pronunciations for these endings, because all three endings for *je, tu, il, elle, ils* and *elles* – *ais/ait/aient* – are pronounced the same.

Il se levait à six heures tous les matins.
Every morning he got up/used to get up/would get up at exactly 6 o'clock.

Parfois mon mari regardait les jeux télévisés avec moi.
Sometimes my husband used to/would watch the game shows with me.

Dans le temps ma grand-mère achetait tous ses cadeaux chez Harrods.
Years ago, my grandmother used to buy all her presents at Harrods.

Nous encouragions nos enfants à apprendre un peu plus de français chaque fois que nous allions en France.
We used to encourage our children to learn more French every time we went to France.

Mes fils insistaient sur ça.
My sons kept insisting on that.

J'apportais des bonbons aux enfants de mon amie.
I used to give sweets to my friend's children.

Elle donnait toujours une cigarette ou une pièce aux sans-abri.
She would always give homeless men or women a cigarette
or a coin.

Tu agissais toujours avant de réfléchir.
You always used to act before thinking.

Ils sortaient tous les samedis.
They used to go out every Saturday.

Elles demandaient la même question toutes les dix minutes.
They kept asking the same question every ten minutes.

Il donnait du muguet à toutes ses soeurs le premier mai.
He used to give lily of the valley to all his sisters on the first
of May.

Ils allaient souvent au théâtre avant d'avoir les enfants.
They used to go to the theatre a lot before they had the
children.

Ils envoyaient des mels.
They kept sending emails.

*Quand les chiens étaient des chiots, ils mordaient nos
pantoufles.*
When the dogs were puppies, they would bite our slippers.

Grand-père réparait nos vélos.
Grandad used to repair our bikes.

Les gens organisaient des fêtes dans la rue.
People used to organise street parties.

On oubliait toujours de leur envoyer une carte.
We always forgot to send them a card.

Tu insultais ma soeur régulièrement.
You insulted my sister regularly.

Elle rentrait toujours fatiguée.
She always came home tired.

Leur père faisait de l'haltérophilie.
Their father used to do weight lifting.

* * *

Il pleuvait toujours pour mon anniversaire.
It always used to rain on my birthday.

Il prenait un bain à la même heure tous les matins.
He would have a bath at the same time every morning.

Tous les dimanches on allait à l'église.
Every Sunday we used to go to church.

Pendant mon enfance je rêvais toujours d'aller en Angleterre.
I used to dream about going to England when I was a child.

Elle rougissait chaque fois.
She would blush every single time.

Elles répétaient les même conseils chaque fois.
They kept on repeating the same advice every time.

On dépensait trop d'argent.
We would spend too much money.

Elle téléphonait tous les soirs.
She kept phoning every night.

Elle appelait son chat à la même heure tous les jours.
She would call her cat in at the same time every day.

Ma mère apportait de la confiture maison lorsqu'elle venait.
My mother used to bring home-made jam when she came.

* * *

Je n'avais pas les moyens de me payer un ordinateur en ce temps là.
I couldn't afford to buy a computer then.

Quand on habitait dans le Berkshire, ma soeur travaillait dans une banque.
When we lived in Berkshire, my sister worked in a bank.

Quand j'étais adolescente, je voulais six enfants.
When I was a teenager, I wanted six children.

C'était le meilleur dentiste du quartier.
He was the best dentist in the area.

Nous avions froid dans cette vieille tente.
We were cold in that old tent.

Les enfants dormaient.
The children were asleep.

Il faisait soleil?
Was the sun shining?

C'était leur tour de conduire.
It was their turn to drive.

Les prix étaient élevés cette année-là.
Prices were high that year.

Je croyais toujours mon ami en ce temps-là.
I always believed my friend in those days.

Le temps était médiocre hier.
The weather was poor yesterday.

Pourquoi est-ce que tu avais faim?
Why were you hungry?

Ils avaient une idée fixe.
They had a set idea.

C'était leur fille préférée.
She was their favourite daughter.

Il faisait chaud dans ce magasin.
It was hot in that shop.

Elle avait mal à la tête.
She had a headache.

Il avait les cheveux blonds quand il était petit.
He had blond hair when he was young.

Le professeur portait un costume noir, et avait l'air d'être très content de lui.
The teacher was wearing a black suit, and looked very pleased with himself.

Elles étaient allemandes.
They were German.

Nous étions inquiets lorsque tu partais faire de l'escalade.
We were worried about you when you went rock climbing.

Elle voulait tout quitter.
She wanted to leave everything.

* * *

On espérait jusqu'à la dernière minute.
We hoped to the end.

Ils voulaient voir d'eux-mêmes.
They wanted to see for themselves.

J'étais stupéfaite.
I was staggered.

Ils voulaient y assister.
They wanted to be there.

C'était fatigant?
Was it tiring?

On pensait le contraire.
We thought the opposite.

Elle semblait effrayée.
She seemed frightened.

Il y avait toujours beaucoup de fleurs dans son jardin.
There always were lots of flowers in his/her garden.

J'avais honte de mes notes d'anglais.
I was ashamed of my English marks.

Vous aviez peur de la réaction de votre chef?
Were you scared of your boss's reaction?

C'était une mauvaise période pour eux.
It was a terrible time for them.

Elle avait beaucoup d'idées lorsqu' elle était jeune.
She had lots of ideas when she was young.

Est-ce que c'était une voiture fiable?
Was it a reliable car?

Il y avait des crêpes pour le dessert.
There were pancakes for pudding.

*Avant le tremblement de terre, des millions de touristes
venaient chaque année.*
Before the earthquake millions of tourists used to come
every year.

Elles étaient contentes d'apprendre la nouvelle.
They were pleased to hear the news.

Je connaissais sa cousine.
I knew his/her cousin.

Quand j'étais jeune, je fumais.
When I was young I used to smoke.

Leurs chiens détestaient le chat du voisin.
Their dogs hated the neighbours' cat.

Nous collectionnions les timbres lorsque nous étions petites.
We used to collect stamps when we were little.

*Est-ce que vous attrapiez beaucoup de poissons quand vous
alliez à la pêche?*
Did you use to catch a lot of fish when you went fishing?

* * *

La maison était jaune.
The house was yellow.

Le château était impressionnant.
The castle was impressive.

Il y avait beaucoup de photos dans le salon.
There were lots of photographs in the lounge.

C'était déjà minuit.
It was already midnight.

L'église était sur une colline.
The church was on a hill.

La clôture était cassée.
The fence was broken.

Leur première voiture était verte.
Their first car was green.

Le camping avait deux étoiles.
The campsite had two stars.

La maison de mon amie était très vieille.
My friend's house was very old.

Il y avait au moins cent personnes à la réunion.
There were at least one hundred people at the meeting.

Notre cuisine était petite.
Our kitchen was small.

Il faisait nuageux.
It was cloudy.

Il y avait souvent des embouteillages aux heures de pointe.
There often were traffic jams at peak times.

Il y avait un pommier ici.
There used to be an apple tree here.

Il faisait nuit et il faisait froid.
It was dark and cold.

Tous les volets des maisons étaient fermés.
All the shutters on the houses were closed.

La rue était déserte.
The street was deserted.

Il y avait un bidet dans leur salle de bain.
There used to be a bidet in their bathroom.

C'était mes voisins.
They used to be my neighbours.

C'était moi.
It was me.

* * *

Il y avait de la musique.
There was music.

Le ciel était bleu.
The sky was blue.

Il était tard.
It was late.

Tout était silencieux.
Everything was quiet.

C'était triste.
It was sad.

C'était excellent.
It was excellent.

C'était bizarre.
It was very strange.

C'était affreux.
It was horrible.

C'était ridicule.
It was ridiculous.

C'était difficile.
It was difficult.

* * *

C'était un dentiste (also Il était dentiste).
He was a dentist.

C'était une chanteuse (also Elle était chanteuse).
She was a singer.

C'était sa femme.
She was his wife.

C'était le curé.
He was the priest.

C'était un imbécile.
He was an idiot.

C'était ses amis.
They were his/her friends.

* * *

C'était un grand jour.
It was an important day.

C'était une erreur.
It was a mistake.

C'était un mardi.
It was a Tuesday.

C'était un petit bateau.
It was a small boat.

C'était un problème.
It was a problem.

C'était un miracle.
It was a miracle.

* * *

Il y avait beaucoup de monde en ville hier.
There were lots of people in town yesterday.

Il y avait une belle vue de l'hôtel.
There was a lovely view from the hotel.

Il y avait des lapins vivants au marché.
There were live rabbits at the market.

Il y avait trop de problèmes.
There were too many problems.

Dans la maison de mes grands-parents il y avait une cave.
In my grandparents' house there was a cellar.

Il y avait un grand choix de livres.
There was a good choice of books.

(Avant) il y avait un cinéma dans ma rue.
There used to be a cinema in my street.

(Avant) il y avait un grand platane devant l'immeuble.
There used to be a large plane tree in front of the block of flats.

(Avant) il y avait une cheminée dans cette pièce.
There used to be a fireplace in this room.

(Avant) il y avait seulement une école dans le village.
There used to be only one school in the village.

(Avant) il y avait une usine près d'ici.
There used to be a factory near here.

(Avant) il y avait toujours une tarte aux pommes le dimanche.
There always used to be apple tart on Sundays.

* * *

Je traversais/j'étais en train de traverser la rue (quand j'ai vu Roxanne).
I was crossing the street (when I saw Roxanne).

Elles dormaient toujours/elles étaient en train de dormir à onze heures!
They were still asleep at eleven!

Il travaillait/était en train de travailler à onze heures du soir samedi dernier.
He was working at eleven o'clock in the evening last Saturday.

Il lisait/était en train de lire (quand tu as téléphoné).
He was reading (when you phoned).

Les enfants buvaient/étaient en train de boire de la limonade.
The children were drinking lemonade.

Il finissait/était en train de finir son repas.
He was finishing his meal.

Ils regardaient un film à minuit.
They were watching a film at midnight.

Je quittais la maison (quand mon portable a sonné).
I was leaving the house when my mobile rang.

Il s'habillait en se dépêchant.
He was dressing in a hurry.

Vous voyagiez plus avant votre mariage?
Did you travel more before your marriage?

Ils fumaient (quand je suis entré/e).
They were smoking (when I came in).

La neige fondait déjà.
The snow was already melting.

On roulait trop vite.
We were travelling too fast.

Elle écoutait la radio.
She was listening to the radio.

Ils partaient (lorsque je suis arrivé/e).
They were leaving (when I arrived).

Je réfléchissais.
I was thinking.

Qu'est-ce que vous disiez à ma femme?
What were you saying to my wife?

Elle rêvait.
She was dreaming.

Nous faisions les lits.
We were making the beds.

Il pleuvait hier.
It was raining yesterday.

* * *

Elle dessinait dans sa chambre.
She was drawing in her bedroom.

Qu'est-ce qu'ils faisaient?
What were they doing?

Qui riait?
Who was laughing?

Elles fabriquaient des cartes pour la fête des mères à l'école.
They were making Mother's Day cards at school.

Qu'est-ce qu'ils construisaient?
What were they building?

Elle se vernissait les ongles.
She was painting her nails.

Quelqu'un gémissait de douleur dehors.
Someone was moaning in pain outside.

Elle se coiffait.
She was combing her hair.

* * *

Si je gagnais à la loterie, j'achèterais une résidence secondaire en France.
If I won the lottery, I would buy a holiday home in France.

S'ils pouvaient, ils changeraient beaucoup de choses.
If they could, they would change a lot of things.

Qu'est-ce que tu dirais si nous changions d'avis?
What would you say if we changed our minds?

Vous pleureriez si je partais?
Would you cry if I left?

On serait content si elle venait.
We would be pleased if she came.

S'il demandait, nous accepterions.
If he were to ask, we would accept.

Ils comprendraient certainement si on expliquait la situation.
They would probably understand if we explained the situation.

Tu le ferais si tu étais libre?
Would you do it if you were free?

Elles viendraient si elles voulaient.
They would come if they wanted to.

Si j'avais le temps, je voyagerais plus.
If I had the time I would travel more.

Si j'étais toi, je divorcerais.
If I were you I would get divorced.

Si je pouvais, je le ferais.
If I could I would do it.

Si elle prêtait son vélo à son frère elle le regretterait.
If she lent her brother her bike, she would regret it.

S'ils avaient l'argent, ils achèteraient un camping car.
If they had the money, they would buy a motorhome.

Ça me serait insupportable si ma fille partait habiter à l'étranger.
I would hate it if my daughter went to live abroad.

Cela vous dérangerait si nous nous garions ici?
Would you mind if we parked here?

Elle louerait une maison si elle allait habiter à Londres?
Would she rent a house if she went to live in London?

Les chiens détesteraient ça si on les mettait en pension pour chiens.
The dogs would hate it if we were to put them in kennels.

Comment tu te débrouillerais si tu étais licencié?
How would you manage if you were made redundant?

Nous le dirions si nous étions contrariés/es.
If we were upset we would say so.

Si on offrait le poste à Nice à mon mari, il refuserait.
If they offered my husband the post in Nice, he would turn it down.

Si tu venais on pourrait jouer au tennis.
If you came we could play tennis.

Si elle voulait elle pourrait faire mieux.
She could do better if she wanted to (if she tried).

* * *

Si seulement j'avais l'argent.....
If only I had the money...

Si seulement tu étais là....
If only you were here...

Si seulement elle pouvait venir....
If only she could come...

Si seulement c'était faisable.
If only it were possible...

Si seulement c'était vrai....
If only it were true...

Si seulement tu étais plus jeune....
If only you were younger...

* * *

Et si on allait au cinéma dimanche?
What about going to the cinema/Shall we go to the cinema?

Et si on refusait?
What if we refused?

Et si nous mangions au restaurant ce soir?
What about eating out tonight?

Et si je téléphonais demain?
What if I phoned tomorrow?

Et si on essayait?
What if we tried/Shall we try?

Et s'il pleuvait?
What if it rains?

Et s'ils étaient malades?
What if they were ill?

Et si tu avais tort?
What if you were wrong?

Et si c'était vrai?
What if it was true?

* * *

On a dit que nous nous ennuyions.
We said that we were bored.

J'ai dit que j'avais trois petits-enfants.
I said that I had three grandchildren.

Ils m'ont demandé si j'avais le temps de venir samedi.
I was asked whether I had time to come on Saturday.

Nous avons dit que nous devions partir à six heures.
We said that we must leave at six.

Elle a dit à ses parents qu'elle était malade.
She told her parents that she was ill.

J'ai dit que j'aimais jouer aux échecs.
I said that I enjoyed playing chess.

Ils ont dit qu'ils étaient irlandais.
They said that they were Irish.

Vous avez dit que vous connaissiez ma mère?
Did you say that you knew my mother?

J'ai prévenu mon patron que j'avais des problèmes avec mon ordinateur.
I told my boss that I had problems with my computer.

Elles ont annoncé qu'elles voulaient intervenir.
They said that they wanted to get involved.

Nous avons dit que nous déménagions en février.
We said that we were moving house in February.

Il a dit à mon ami qu'il était marié.
He told my friend that he was married.

On a dit que nous avions deux frères qui travaillaient à l'étranger.
We said that we had two brothers working abroad.

Ils ont insisté qu'ils devaient partir lundi.
They insisted that they must leave on Monday.

Il a demandé aux enfants s'ils savaient parler le français.
He asked the children whether they could speak French.

Elle a dit qu'elle voulait revenir.
She said that she wanted to come again.

Vous avez mentionné que vous pouviez garantir une date.
You mentioned that you could guarantee a date.

J'ai dit que j'avais un nouveau portable.
I said that I had a new mobile phone.

Il a demandé si la voiture marchait bien.
He asked if the car went well/was going well.

Il a informé le personnel que tout le monde devait faire des heures supplémentaires aujourd'hui.
He informed the staff that everyone had to work overtime today.

* * *

A onze heures la reine arrivait à la cathédrale pour les obsèques de sa mère.
At eleven, the Queen arrived at the cathedral for her mother's funeral.

En 1995 le couple célèbre divorçait.
In 1995, the famous couple divorced.

Le 3 mai 1965, le chanteur naissait.
On the third of May 1965, the singer was born.

A huit heures l'avion atterrissait comme prévu.
At eight, the plane landed as expected.

Le lendemain la presse annonçait la démission du président.
The next day, the press announced the President's resignation.

A l'aube, le bateau chavirait.
At dawn, the boat capsized.

Cette année-là il réussissait sa licence en droit.
That year, he was to finish his law degree.

Ce matin-là la compagnie annonçait la faillite.
That morning, the company announced bankruptcy.

> ■ There are some minor spelling peculiarities for pronunciation purposes with verbs ending in '__ger' or '__cer.'
> ➤ Verbs ending in '__ger' have an '**e**' inserted in front of the imperfect endings for 'I,' 'he,' 'she,' 'it' and 'they'. This softens the letter 'g' before the 'a' of the endings:

*Il neig**e**ait?*
Was it snowing?

*Ça chang**e**ait tout.*
It changed everything.

*Ils décharg**e**aient le camion.*
They were unloading the lorry.

*Tu mang**e**ais?*
Were you eating?

*On nag**e**ait dans la rivière.*
We used to swim in the river.

*Elles partag**e**aient une chambre.*
They used to share a room.

*Je rang**e**ais le salon.*
I was tidying the lounge.

*Il boug**e**ait toute la nuit.*
He used to toss and turn all night.

Je dérangeais toujours ma copine.
I always used to put my friend out.

Ils encourageaient leurs petits-enfants.
They would encourage their grandchildren.

Je mélangeais tout.
I used to/would mix everything up.

Il obligeait ses enfants à y aller.
He used to make his children go.

Ça prolongeait le suspense.
That prolonged the suspense.

Ils voyageaient beaucoup plus.
They used to travel far more.

Elle plongeait bien.
She used to dive really well.

Naturellement, ils protégeaient leurs intérêts.
Naturally they were protecting their interests.

Les rats rongeaient les boîtes en carton.
Rats kept gnawing the cardboard boxes.

Et si on déménageait?
What about moving house/What if we were to move house?

Elle se chargeait toujours de ça.
She always used to sort all that out.

Ça prolongeait le travail.
It used to make more work.

> ➤ Similarly, with verbs ending in '__cer,' a **cedilla** is added to the letter '**c**' of the 'I,' 'he,' 'she,' 'it' and 'they' forms. The adjustment softens the letter 'c' before the 'a' of the imperfect endings:

Je renonçais à l'avance.
I would/used to give up in advance.

La même année il divorçait.
He got divorced the same year.

Elle devançait ses parents chaque fois.
Every time she would/used to beat her parents to it.

Le camion avançait lentement.
The lorry was approaching slowly.

Elles commençaient très tôt.
They would/used to start very early.

Je me forçais.
I would/used to force myself.

Ça influençait les décisions.
It used to influence decisions.

Ils annonçaient toujours les résultats le même jour.
They would always announce the results on the same day.

Elle balançait son sac dans le salon.
She used to throw her bag in the lounge.

Je suçais toujours mon pouce à cinq ans!
I was still sucking my thumb aged five!

Il fronçait toujours les sourcils.
He always frowned.

On commençait toujours en retard.
We always used to start late.

Je m'avançais vers la place (quand j'ai entendu la sirène).
I was walking towards the square (when I heard the alarm).

Il berçait le chaton.
He was gently rocking the kitten.

On plaçait les coussins sur les lits.
We used to put the cushions on the beds.

Helping you learn

Progress questions

1. What are the rules governing the formation of the imperfect tense?
2. Check your answer.

Discussion points

Discuss differences between the two languages with anyone who shares this interest.

Practical assignment

1. Translate some of the French and English examples in the different sections.
2. Check your answers.

Study tips

Practise your French at every opportunity.

9

More on the Perfect and Imperfect

As is the case in English, the most commonly used tenses when talking about the past in conversation are the perfect and the imperfect .

The perfect describes what happened, what occurred, but the imperfect can add other details to these actions, such as descriptions. The imperfect tense can be used to describe unfinished, continuous actions, including things that used to take place as well as things that existed already, such as descriptions.

(From this point on, the infinitive of the verbs that have an irregular past participle are no longer given.)

■ All the verbs in the following paragraph are in the perfect (the speaker is female).

Cette année pendant les grandes vacances **je suis allée** en France sur la Côte d'Azur, exactement à Boulouris, près de Saint-Raphaël, avec mon mari et ma fille (malheureusement **il a fallu** mettre notre chien en pension pour animaux). Nous **avons pris** le taxi de chez nous à l'aéroport. Puis **nous avons pris** l'avion pour Nice, le vol **a duré** une heure et demie seulement. A Nice **on a marché** jusqu'à la petite gare pas loin de l'aéroport, et **nous sommes arrivés** à Saint-Raphaël en train. Ensuite **nous avons décidé** de prendre un taxi pour aller au camping. **Nous avons passé** une agréable quinzaine. **Nous nous sommes reposés, nous nous sommes promenés, nous nous sommes baignés, nous nous sommes fait bronzer, nous avons visité** les alentours. **Nous avons eu** beaucoup de chance parce qu'**il a fait** très beau et très chaud tous les jours. **Nous sommes rentrés** en pleine forme.

This year in the summer holidays **I went** to France on the Côte d'Azur, to Boulouris, near Saint-Raphaë,l with my husband and my daughter (unfortunately **we had** to put our dog in kennels). **We went** to the airport by taxi. Then **we flew** to Nice, **the flight took** only one and a half hours. In Nice **we walked** to the small station not far from the airport, and **we arrived** in Saint-Raphaël by train. After that **we decided** to take a taxi to the campsite. **We enjoyed** a lovely fortnight. **We rested, we went for walks, we went swimming, we sunbathed** and **we went sightseeing** in the area. **We were** very lucky because the weather **was** very good and very hot every day. **We returned home** very fit.

■ All the verbs in the following paragraph are in the imperfect (the speaker is male).

Quand **j'étais** petit **j'habitais** dans une petite ville en Normandie. Dans ma ville **il** y **avait** plusieurs petites épiceries, pas self-service, **il** n'y **avait** pas de supermarchés. **Le propriétaire** de l'épicerie de notre quartier **était** assez vieux, grand et mince et **il avait** une petite moustache. **Il sentait** toujours le tabac. **On avait** une maison près de l'église. **Mon grand-père habitait** avec nous. **Il** me **racontait** souvent son enfance. **Mon père cultivait** beaucoup de légumes dans notre petit jardin. Le dimanche **j'aidais** maman à faire la cuisine, ça me **plaisait**. **J'avais** un chat noir, **il s'appelait** Réglisse, **il était** coquin. **J'adorais** mon chat. **J'allais** à l'école à pied, **c'était** pas loin, et de toutes façons, **mes parents** n'**avaient** pas de voiture. A l'école **j'avais** deux meilleurs amis. **J'aimais** l'orthographe, mais **je détestais** l'histoire et **j'étais** nul en calcul. Pendant les vacances, **j'allais** souvent en Angleterre chez ma tante. **Elle était** mariée à un Anglais. **Elle** n'**avait** pas d'enfants, et **je m'ennuyais** un peu. **J'écrivais** beaucoup de lettres à maman et papa. En Angleterre, **je** n'**aimais** pas le thé ou la gelée (au fruit), mais **j'adorais** les chips au poulet.

When **I was** young **I used to live** in a small town in Normandy. In my town **there used to be** several small food shops, **there were**n't any supermarkets. **The owner** of the local grocer's shop **was** quite old, tall and thin, and **he had** a small moustache. **He** always **smelt** of tobacco. **We had** a house near the church. **My grandfather used to live** with us. **He** often **used to talk** to me about his childhood. **My father used to grow** a lot of vegetables in our little garden. On Sundays **I used to help** Mum with the cooking, **I enjoyed** it. **I used to have** a black cat, **his name was** Réglisse (liquorice), **he was** cheeky. **I did love** my cat. **I used to walk** to school, **it was**n't far, and in any case **my parents did** not **have** a car. At school **I had** two best friends. **I used to enjoy** spelling but **I hated** history, and **I was** rubbish at sums. During the holidays I often **used to go** to my aunt's in England. **She was** married to an Englishman. **She did**n't **have** children and **I used to get** a bit **bored**. **I used to write** a lot of letters to mum and dad. In England, **I did** not **like** tea or jelly, but **I loved** chicken-flavour crisps.

■ Both the perfect and imperfect tenses are used in the following paragraph (the speaker is female).

Hier **je suis allée** en ville, parce que **j'avais besoin** d'aller à la banque. **Il était** environ une heure quand **je suis partie**. **Il y avait** beaucoup de circulation. **Je me suis garée** derrière le cinéma. **Il faisait** vraiment trop chaud dans les magasins et **il y avait** beaucoup de monde. **J'ai trouvé** une nouvelle petite boutique où **j'ai acheté** des boucles d'oreille pour l'anniversaire de ma fille. Après environ deux heures, comme **j'avais soif**, **je me suis payé** une tasse de thé et **j'ai pris** une tarte à la crème. **Elle était** délicieuse. Après **j'ai continué** avec mes courses. **J'ai vu** une jolie robe rouge **qui** n'**était** pas chère. **Je** l'**ai essayée**, mais **je** ne l'**ai** pas **achetée** parce qu'**elle** ne m'**allait** pas bien. **J'ai regardé** les chaussures parce qu'**elles étaient** en solde. Toutes **les pointures étaient** trop petites pour moi. **Je suis rentrée** vers cinq heures. **J'étais** fatiguée. **Il faisait** déjà nuit. Malheureusement **j'ai oublié** d'aller à la banque!

Yesterday **I went** to town because **I needed** to go to the bank. **It was** about one o'clock when **I left**. **There was** a lot of traffic. **I parked the car** behind the cinema. It really **was** too hot in the shops, and **they were** crowded. **I found** a new boutique where **I bought** some earrings for my daughter's birthday. After about two hours **I was** thirsty, so **I treated myself** to a cup of tea and **I had** a cream tart. **It was** delicious. After that, **I carried on** with my shopping. **I saw** a pretty red dress, **which was** not expensive. **I tried** it **on** but **I did**n't **buy** it because **it did**n't **suit** me. **I looked** at the shoes because **they were** on sale. All **the sizes were** too small for me. **It was** already dark when **I got back** around five. **I was** tired. Unfortunately, **I forgot** to go to the bank!

> ■ As in English, the imperfect tense is usually found in combination with the perfect tense. Below are more examples:

J'ai passé mon permis de conduire quand j'habitais à Londres.
I took my driving test when I lived in London.

Ma fille était malade, alors nous nous sommes occupés de nos petits-enfants.
My daughter was ill so we looked after our grandchildren.

J'ai ouvert la lettre parce qu'elle avait l'air intéressante.
I opened the letter because it looked interesting.

Il faisait si froid que j'ai mis trois paires de chaussettes.
It was so cold that I put on three pairs of socks.

Mon cousin est mort quand il avait cinquante ans.
My cousin died when he was fifty.

Quand j'ai vu ton frère il traversait la place.
When I saw your brother he was crossing the square.

Ils couraient à toute allure quand la pluie s'est arrêtée.
They were running like mad when the rain stopped.

Elle a suivi le chemin qui allait au sommet de la colline.
She followed the path that went to the top of the hill.

Tu étais chez toi lorsque ça s'est passé?
Were you at home when that happened?

J'avais si faim que j'ai mangé la moitié de la baguette.
I was so hungry that I ate half the baguette.

Il était minuit quand l'orage est survenu.
It was midnight when the storm broke.

Vous avez bâti la serre pendant qu'ils se reposaient?
Did you build the greenhouse whilst they were resting?

Elle a découvert la vérité lorsqu'elle était chez nous.
She discovered the truth when she was staying with us.

J'avais besoin d'argent donc je suis allée à la banque.
I needed some money, so I went to the bank.

On a compris que cela gênait mes beaux-parents.
We understood that it made my parents-in-law feel
uncomfortable.

Elle a dit qu'elle traversait une période difficile.
She said that she was going through a difficult period.

■ Sometimes, as is the case in English, there is a slight
variation in meaning depending on the tense used:

Soudain j'ai été/étais inquiète.
Suddenly I got/was worried.

Tu as eu/avais tort de crier.
You have been/were wrong to shout.

Elle a été/était très en colère.
She has been/was very cross.

Il a été/était très gêné quand elle a dit ça.
He was embarrassed when she said that.

Ils ont eu/avaient l'air triste.
They looked sad.

Il a fallu/fallait parler à mon patron tout de suite.
I needed to talk to my boss immediately.

Tu as eu/avais honte de tes résultats?
Were you ashamed of your results?

J'ai été/étais très émue lorsque j'ai vu la maison.
I was very moved when I saw the house.

Mon fils a eu/avait raison de partir.
My son was right to leave.

Il a eu/avait peur.
He has been/got scared.

* * *

Nous avons été/nous étions stupides de croire son histoire.
We have been/we were stupid to believe this story.

Après cinq heures, les enfants ont eu/avaient faim.
After five the children got/were hungry.

Les animaux ont eu/avaient trop chaud cet été.
The animals got/were too hot this summer.

C'est alors que ça a été/c'était un problème.
Then it was a problem.

Puis il a fallu/fallait partir.
So, we had to go.

Il y a eu/avait beaucoup de questions.
There were many questions.

Après cela la rue a été/était silencieuse.
After that the street was quiet.

* * *

La vendeuse a été/était gentille hier.
The shop assistant was helpful yesterday.

Quand j'ai eu/avais vingt ans, j'ai décidé d'acheter une voiture.
When I was (turned) twenty I decided to buy a car.

Nous avons voulu/voulions faire une différence.
We wanted to make a difference.

C'est ce qu'elle a pensé/pensait.
That's what she thought/was thinking.

Elle a eu envie/avait envie d'aller au cinéma.
She fancied going to the cinema.

Vous avez été/étiez plutôt naïf.
You have been/were rather naïve.

Tu as eu/avais l'air contente quand le téléphone a sonné.
You looked happy when the phone rang.

Seulement mon père a compris/comprenait mon frère.
Only my father understood/used to understand my brother.

Il a eu/avait l'air contrarié.
He has looked/looked upset.

Ça a été/c'était impossible.
It has been/was impossible.

J'ai voulu/voulais parler au professeur hier.
I wanted to speak to the teacher yesterday.

Elles ont pensé/pensaient que ce serait mieux.
They thought that it would be better.

* * *

J'ai fumé/je fumais (quand j'étais adolescent).
I smoked/used to smoke (when I was a teenager).

Ça a été/c'était toute une histoire.
It has been/was quite an upset.

Elle a voulu/voulait voir.
She wanted to see.

Il y a eu/avait beaucoup de vent ici l'autre jour.
There has been a lot of wind here/there was a lot of wind here the other day.

Elles ont été/étaient tristes.
They have been/were sad.

J'ai été malade/étais malade.
I have been/was ill.

Il a plu/pleuvait hier.
It rained/has rained/did rain/was raining yesterday.

Il a été en colère/était en colère toute la semaine.
He has been/was cross all week.

Nous avons été injustes/étions injustes de croire ça.
We have been/were unfair to believe that.

Est-ce qu'il a pu/pouvait se payer des vacances l'an passé?
Has he been able to/could he afford a holiday last year?

Tu as eu/avais mal à la tête?
Have you had/did you have a headache?

Vous avez eu/aviez beaucoup de doutes?
Have you had/did you have many doubts?

Est-ce qu'il a fallu/fallait qu'il fasse tout le ménage lui même?
Did he have to do all the housework himself?

> ■ If, on the other hand, only one of the two tenses can be correctly used, usage is dictated by the <u>exact context</u> (depending on what is said before, what is said after, or both). As a guide, when the English simple past can <u>equally</u> be replaced by the perfect tense, then only the perfect tense is correct in French. When the simple tense can <u>equally</u> be replaced with 'used to', then the imperfect tense must be used:

Il y avait un bouchon tous les lundis à ce carrefour.
There was (used to be) a traffic jam every Monday at this crossroads.

Malheureusement, il y a eu un accident.
Sadly, there was (has been) an accident.

Je voyais ma nièce régulièrement à cette époque-là.
I saw (used to see) my niece regularly then.

J'ai vu mon cousin deux fois dans ce restaurant.
I saw (have seen) my cousin twice in this restaurant.

C'était ta faute.
It was (used to be) your fault.

Encore une fois, ça a été ma faute.
It was (has been) my fault again.

Elle avait une angine chaque hiver quand elle habitait dans cette ville.
She had (used to have) tonsillitis every winter when she lived (used to live) in that town.

Elle avait quatre ans quand elle a eu les oreillons.
She was four when she had (did have) the mumps.

Il détestait la mer.
He hated (used to hate) the sea.

Il a détesté le spectacle.
He hated (has hated) the show.

Nous avions un magasin à Biarritz.
We had (used to have) a shop in Biarritz.

Nous avons eu plusieurs magasins pendant cette période.
We had (did have) several shops during that time.

Je mangeais beaucoup de bonbons.
I ate (used to eat) a lot of sweets.

J'ai mangé chez mon frère hier soir.
I ate (did eat) at my brother's house last night.

Pendant la guerre Noël était plutôt triste.
During the war Christmas was (used to be) rather sad.

Noël a été plutôt triste l'an passé.
Christmas was rather sad last year.

Tu pleurais à tous les coups.
You cried (used to cry) each time.

Tu as pleuré encore une fois?
You cried (did cry) again?

Helping you learn

Progress questions

1. Summarise the differences between these two past tenses.
2. Give examples of when using either tense might convey the same meaning.
3. Give contrasting examples where using one or the other tense might convey a slightly different meaning.

Discussion points

1. Discuss differences between the two tenses with fellow students, as well as anyone else interested in the subject.
2. Discuss grey areas, when one of two tenses could be correct.

Practical assignment

1. Write about your last holiday in French.
2. Discuss with fellow students and anyone else interested in the subject.

> **Study tips**
> Think, read, write, speak in French and listen to at least a little French every day.

10

Agreement of Past Participles with 'Avoir'

One-minute overview

Past participles of verbs that take *avoir* in the perfect tense agree in gender and number with its direct object when this direct object precedes the verb (which, unlike in English, is always the case in French when the direct object is a pronoun):

■ There is no change to the past participle when the direct object is masculine singular:

*J'ai aimé **Antoine**. Je l'ai aimé.*
I liked Antoine. I liked him.

*J'ai acheté **un sac**. Je l'ai acheté.*
I bought a bag. I bought it.

***Le sac** que j'ai acheté est en cuir.*
The bag I bought is made of leather.

*J'ai mangé **le sandwich**. Je l'ai mangé.*
I ate the sandwich. I ate it.

***Le sandwich** que j'ai mangé était au jambon.*
The sandwich I ate was a ham sandwich.

*Nous avons mis **le plan** sur la table. Nous l'avons mis sur la table.*
We have put the street map on the table. We have put it on the table.

■ An 'e' is added to the past participle when the direct object is feminine singular:

*J'ai aimé **Stéphanie**. Je l'ai aimée.*
I liked Stéphanie. I liked her.

*J'ai acheté **une robe**. Je l'ai achetée.*
I bought a dress. I bought it.

***La robe** que j'ai achetée est verte.*
The dress I bought is green.

*J'ai mangé **la glace**. Je l'ai mangée.*
I ate the ice cream. I ate it.

***La glace** que j'ai mangée était italienne.*
The ice cream I ate was Italian.

*Nous avons mis **la carte** sur l'étagère. Nous l'avons mise sur l'étagère.*
We have put the road map on the shelf. We have put it on the shelf.

NOTE: Feminine agreement of a past participle will only vary slightly in pronunciation if the past participle ends with a consonant, when this results in an extra syllable.

■ An 's' is added to the past participle when the direct object is masculine plural, or when it refers to both masculine and feminine:

*J'ai aimé **Antoine et Claude**. Je **les** ai aimés.*
I loved Antoine and Claude. I loved them.

*J'ai aimé **Antoine et Stéphanie**. Je **les** ai aimés.*
I loved Antoine and Stéphanie. I loved them.

*J'ai acheté **deux sacs**. Je **les** ai achetés.*
I bought two bags. I bought them.

***Les deux sacs** que j'ai achetés sont en tissus.*
The two bags I have bought are made of material.

*J'ai acheté **un sac et une robe**. Je **les** ai achetés.*
I bought a bag and a dress. I bought them.

***Le sac et la robe** que j'ai achetés sont dans l'armoire.*
The bag and the dress I bought are in the wardrobe.

*J'ai mangé **les sandwiches**. Je **les** ai mangés.*
I have eaten the sandwiches. I have eaten them.

*J'ai mangé **le sandwich et la glace**. Je **les** ai mangés.*
I have eaten the sandwich and the ice cream. I have eaten them.

*Nous avons mis **les plans** dans une enveloppe. Nous **les** avons mis dans une enveloppe.*
We have put the street maps in an envelope. We have put them in an envelope.

*Nous avons mis **le plan et la carte** ici. Nous **les** avons mis ici.*
We have put the street map and the road map here. We have put them here.

■ The feminine plural ending is 'es':

*J'ai aimé **Valérie et Stéphanie**. Je **les** ai aimées.*
I liked Valérie and Stéphanie. I liked them.

*J'ai acheté **deux robes**. Je **les** ai achetées.*
I bought two dresses. I bought them.

***Les deux robes** que j'ai achetées étaient plutôt chères.*
The two dresses I have bought were rather expensive.

*J'ai mangé **les glaces**. Je **les** ai mangées.*
I have eaten the ice creams. I have eaten them.

*Nous avons mis **les cartes** dans la valise. Nous **les** avons mises dans la valise.*
We have put the road maps in the suitcase. We have put them in the suitcase.

■ More mixed examples:

*Le bateau a quitté **le port**. Le bateau **l'**a quitté.*
The boat has left the harbour. The boat has left it.

*Il a gaspillé tout **son argent**. Il **l'**a gaspillé.*
He has wasted all his money. He has wasted it.

*On a oublié **son anniversaire**. On l'a oublié.*
We have forgotten his/her birthday. We have forgotten it.

*Il a laissé **le chien** dehors. Il l'a laissé dehors.*
He left the dog outside. He left him outside.

*Vous avez montré **votre passeport**? Vous l'avez montré?*
Have you shown your passport? Have you shown it?

*Nous avons trouvé **ce bon restaurant** il y a trois ans. Nous l'avons trouvé il y a trois ans.*
We found this good restaurant three years ago. We found it three years ago.

*Elles ont étudié **l'anglais** pendant deux ans. Elles l'ont étudié pendant deux ans.*
They have studied English for two years. They studied it for two years.

*J'ai monté **le livre**. Je l'ai monté.*
I took the book upstairs. I took it upstairs.

*Elle a descendu **le bébé**. Elle l'a descendu.*
She took the baby downstairs. She took him downstairs.

*Ils ont passé **le pont**. Ils l'ont passé.*
They went past the bridge. They went past it.

*Il a monté **le courrier** dans la chambre. Il l'a monté dans la chambre.*
He took the post up to the bedroom. He took it up to the bedroom.

*Où est-ce que vous avez laissé **le parapluie**? Où est-ce que vous l'avez laissé?*
Where did you leave the umbrella? Where did you leave it?

*J'ai félicité **mon petit-fils**. Je l'ai félicité.*
I congratulated my grandson. I congratulated him.

*Tu as fait **le lit**? Tu l'as fait?*
Have you made the bed? Have you made it?

*J'ai donné **mon numéro de téléphone**. Je l'ai donné.*
I gave my telephone number. I gave it.

* * *

*Il a rencontré **Madame Bertrand** devant la laverie. Il l'a rencontrée devant la laverie.*
He met Madame Bertrand outside the launderette. He met her outside the launderette.

*Quand est-ce qu'il a expliqué **la situation**? Quand est-ce qu'il l'a expliquée?*
When did he explain the situation? When did he explain it?

*Mes parents ont vendu **leur tente**. Ils l'ont vendue.*
My parents have sold their tent. They have sold it.

***L'erreur** qu'il a commise n'est pas grave.*
The mistake he made is not serious.

***La décision** qu'ils ont prise est logique.*
The decision they took makes sense.

*Elle a traduit **l'invitation**. Elle l'a traduite.*
She has translated the invitation. She has translated it.

*Le train a quitté **la gare** à une heure. Il l'a quittée à une heure.*
The train left the station at one. It left it at one.

*Ils ont lavé **la voiture**. Ils l'ont lavée.*
They have washed the car. They have washed it.

*Vous avez influencé **la décision** du maire? Vous l'avez influencée?*
Did you influence the mayor's decision? Did you influence it?

*Il s'est coupé **la main**. Il se l'est coupée.*
He has cut his hand. He has cut it.

*J'ai sorti **la poubelle** trop tard. Je l'ai sortie trop tard.*
I took the dustbin out too late. I took it out too late.

*Vous avez vidé **la boîte à lettres**? Vous l'avez vidée?*
Have you emptied the letter box? Have you emptied it?

*Elle a payé **l'addition**. Elle l'a payée.*
She has paid the bill. She has paid it.

*J'ai garé **la voiture** derrière le supermarché. Je l'ai gar**ée** derrière le supermarché.*

I have parked the car behind the supermaket. I have parked it behind the supermarket.

*Je me suis foulé **la cheville** plusieurs fois. Je me **la** suis foul**ée** plusieurs fois.*

I have sprained my ankle several times. I have sprained it several times.

* * *

*Elle a envoyé **les cadeaux**. Elle **les** a envoyé**s**.*
She has sent the presents. She has sent them.

*J'ai mélangé **les ingrédients**. Je **les** ai mélang**és**.*
I have mixed the ingredients up. I have mixed them up.

***Les problèmes** que vous avez découvert**s** sont importants?*
Are the problems you discovered big?

*Ils ont détesté **les feuilletons**. Ils **les** ont détest**és**.*
They hated the soap operas. They hated them.

*Tu as cassé **mes plats**? Tu **les** as cass**és**?*
Have you broken my dishes? Have you broken them?

*Nous avons retourné **les compliments**. Nous **les** avons retourn**és**.*
We have returned the compliments. We have returned them.

*Vous avez partagé **les biscuits**? Vous **les** avez partag**és**?*
Did you share the biscuits? Did you share them?

*J'ai dérangé **les chiots**. Je **les** ai dérang**és**.*
I disturbed the puppies. I disturbed them.

***Les chocolats** qu'il a fait**s** sont délicieux.*
The chocolates he made are delicious.

*J'ai invité **mes amis**. Je **les** ai invit**és**.*
I invited my friends. I invited them.

*Nous avons aimé **les professeurs**. Nous **les** avons aim**és**.*
We have seen the teachers. We have seen them.

*Elle a pendu **les tableaux**. Elle **les** a pend**us**.*
She hung the pictures up. She hung them up.

*Vous avez envoyé **les méls**? Vous **les** avez envoy**és**?*
Did you send the emails? Did you send them?

*Elles ont descendu **les sacs**. Elles **les** ont descend**us**.*
They have taken the bags down. They have taken them down.

*Nous avons retourné **les livres** à la bibliothèque. Nous **les** avons retourn**és**.*
We have returned the books to the library. We have returned them to the library.

* * *

*Vous avez déchiré **les lettres**? Vous **les** avez déchir**ées**?*
Have you torn the letters up? Have you torn them up?

*Il a demandé **les mêmes questions** trois fois. Il **les** a demand**ées** trois fois.*
He asked the same questions three times. He asked them three times.

*J'ai nettoyé **les chambres**. Je **les** ai nettoy**ées**.*
I cleaned the bedrooms. I cleaned them.

***Les raisons** que vous avez donn**ées** sont ridicules.*
The reasons you have given are ridiculous.

*Tu as descendu **les boîtes**? Tu **les** as descend**ues**?*
Have you taken the boxes downstairs? Have you taken them downstairs?

*Tu as rangé **tes affaires**? Tu **les** as rang**ées**?*
Did you tidy up your things? Did you tidy them up?

*On a sorti **les photos** du mariage. On **les** a sort**ies**.*
We got the wedding photos out. We got them out.

*Tu as écrit **les cartes postales**? Tu **les** as écr**ites**?*
Have you written the postcards? Have you written them?

*Ils ont demandé **les adresses**. Ils **les** ont demand**ées**.*
They have asked for the addresses. They have asked for them.

Les remarques qu'ils ont faites sont utiles.
The remarks they made are useful.

Les maisons qu'ils ont construites sont du style provençal.
The houses they built are in the Provençal style.

Vous avez monté les valises dans la mauvaise chambre. Vous les avez montées dans la mauvaise chambre.
You have taken the suitcases up to the wrong bedroom. You have taken them up to the wrong bedroom.

Ils ont rentré les plantes. Ils les ont rentrées.
They have brought the plants in. They have brought them in.

Elles ont mangé les crêpes. Elles les ont mangées.
They have eaten the pancakes. They have eaten them.

Où est-ce que tu a mis les chaises? Où est-ce que tu les a mises?
Where did you put the chairs? Where did you put them?

* * *

J'ai écouté mon fils et ma fille. Je les ai écoutés.
I listened to my son and my daughter. I listened to them.

Nous avons aimé le pont et l'église. Nous les avons aimés.
We like the bridge and the church. We liked them.

Elle a fait un gâteau et une tarte. Elle les a faits.
She has made a cake and a tart. She has made them.

Nous avons envoyé l'argent et la lettre hier. Nous les avons envoyés hier.
We sent the money and the letter yesterday. We sent them yesterday.

La montre et le bracelet que j'ai perdus étaient des cadeaux.
The watch and the necklace I have lost were presents.

J'ai accompagné ma mère et mon père chez le dentiste. Je les ai accompagnés chez le dentiste.
I took my mother and my father to the dentist's. I took them to the dentist's.

*Vous avez fermé **la porte et le portail**? Vous **les** avez fermés?*
Have you closed the door and the gate? Have you closed them?

*Elle a félicité **son frère et sa sœur**. Elle **les** a félicités.*
She has congratulated her brother and her sister. She has congratulated them.

*J'ai choisi **le melon et la galette** aux fruits de mer. Je **les** ai choisis.*
I have chosen the melon and the seafood pancake. I have chosen them.

*Tu as farci **le poulet et la dinde**? Tu **les** as farcis?*
Have you stuffed the chicken and the turkey? Have you stuffed them?

*Ils ont fini **le vin et la bière**. Ils **les** ont finis.*
They have finished the the wine and the beer. They have finished them.

***La boîte et le sac** que j'ai ouverts sont sur le lit.*
The box and the bag that I have opened are on the bed.

*Ils ont puni **leur petit-fils et leur petite-fille**. Ils **les** ont punis.*
They have punished their grandson and their granddaughter. They have punished them.

*J'ai senti **le mimosa et les violettes**. Je **les** ai sentis.*
I smelt the mimosa and the violets. I smelt them.

*Elles ont attendu **leur tante et leur oncle**. Elles **les** ont attendus.*
They waited for their uncle and their aunt. They waited for them.

Helping you learn

Progress questions

1. When does the past participle agree with direct objects?
2. What are the rules for the various agreements?

Discussion points

1. Discuss rules for the agreement of past participles with fellow students and anyone else interested in the subject.
2. Compare with English past participles.

Practical assignment

1. Translate some English and some French examples.
2. Check your answers.

Study tips

1. Read and re-read rules and appropriate examples until you have absorbed the rules.
2. Little and often works well.

The Perfect Tense and Interrogative Forms

Questions in French can be formed in three ways. The first relies on intonation, the second on the insertion of a set phrase before the statement, and the third on a slight change of word order, which in some instances requires the addition of one extra letter. All three methods are interchangeable.

■ The method <u>most commonly employed</u> in everyday conversation is the first: simply raise your voice, inserting an audible question mark at the end of any statement, and it becomes a question (as can be done in English):

Il a déchargé le camion?
Has he unloaded the lorry?

Les pommes ont moisi?
Have the apples rotted?

Elle a grossi?
Has she put on weight?

Nous sommes arrivés trop tôt?
Have we arrived too early?

On a oublié?
Have we forgotten?

Vous avez forcé la serrure?
Did you force the lock?

Tu as choisi la date?
Have you chosen the date?

Il a fermé le magasin?
Did he shut the shop?

On a démoli la vieille école?
Have they demolished the old school?

Il a répondu?
Did he reply?

Tu as réservé les places?
Have you booked the seats?

Les maçons ont pu continuer?
Were the builders able to continue?

Tu es allé à la piscine?
Did you go to the swimming pool?

Nous avons manqué le train?
Have we missed the train?

Les enfants se sont amusés?
Did the children enjoy themselves?

Vous avez dit quelque chose?
Did you say something?

Tu t'es gargarisé tous les soirs?
Did you gargle every night?

Elle a goûté la sauce?
Has she tried the sauce?

Vous vous êtes dépêché?
Did you hurry up?

Nous avons gagné?
Did we win?

On a perdu le pari?
Did we lose the bet?

Tu as boudé?
Did you sulk?

Nous avons commis une erreur?
Have we made a mistake?

Ton mari a regretté?
Was your husband sorry?

J'ai rougi?
Did I blush?

Vous avez attendu longtemps?
Did you wait for a long time?

Je me suis trompé?
Have I made a mistake?

Tu as aidé?
Did you help?

Elle a réfléchi?
Did she give it some thought?

Ils ont crié?
Did they scream?

■ An equally easy method (especially for those who have difficulties raising their voices) is to introduce the phrase '*est-ce que*' (literally 'is it that') in front of any statement, for example:

Est-ce qu'il a déchargé le camion?
Est-ce que les pommes ont moisi?
Est-ce qu'elle a grossi?
Est-ce que nous sommes arrivés trop tôt?
Est-ce qu'on a oublié?
Est-ce que vous avez forcé la serrure?
Est-ce que tu as choisi la date?
Est-ce qu'il a fermé le magasin?
Est-ce qu'on a démoli la vieille école?
Est-ce qu'il a répondu?
Est-ce que tu as réservé les places?
Est-ce que les maçons ont pu continuer?
Est-ce que tu es allé à la piscine?
Est-ce que nous avons manqué le train?

Est-ce que les enfants se sont amusés?
Est-ce que vous avez dit quelque chose?
Est-ce que tu t'es gargarisé tous les soirs?
Est-ce qu'elle a goûté la sauce?
Est-ce que vous vous êtes dépêché?
Est-ce que nous avons gagné?
Est-ce qu'on a perdu le pari?
Est-ce que tu as boudé?
Est-ce que nous avons commis une erreur?
Est-ce que ton mari a regretté?
Est-ce que j'ai rougi?
Est-ce que vous avez attendu longtemps?
Est-ce que je me suis trompé?
Est-ce que tu as aidé?
Est-ce qu'elle a réfléchi?
Est-ce qu'ils ont crié?

NOTE: There is no need to raise your voice when asking questions using '*est-ce que*,' but it does not sound wrong or strange to do so.

■ Finally, as is in the case with English, a question can be formed by reversing the order of the subject pronoun and the verbs 'to have' or 'to be' (now verb and subject, and hyphenated). However, when the subject is a noun, the appropriate subject pronoun also needs to be added. If as a result two vowels are next to one another, the letter 't' is inserted between the verb and the pronoun:

A-t-il déchargé le camion?
Les pommes, ont-elles moisi?
A-t-elle grossi?
Sommes-nous arrivés trop tôt?
A-t-on oublié?
Avez-vous forcé la serrure?
As-tu choisi la date?
A-t-il fermé le magasin?
A-t-on démoli la vieille école?

A-t-il répondu?
As-tu réservé les places?
Les maçons, ont-ils pu continuer?
Es-tu allé à la piscine?
Avons-nous manqué le train?
Se sont-ils amusés, les enfants?
Avez-vous dit quelque chose?
T'es-tu gargarisé tous les soirs?
A-t-elle goûté la sauce?
Vous êtes-vous dépêché?
Avons-nous gagné?
A-t-on perdu le pari?
As-tu boudé?
Avons-nous commis une erreur?
Ton mari, a-t-il regretté?
Ai-je rougi?
Avez-vous attendu longtemps?
Me suis-je trompé?
As-tu aidé?
A-t-elle réfléchi?
Ont-ils crié?

NOTE: Again, there is no need for rising intonation when verb and subject order has been reversed, but it does not sound wrong or strange to do so.

Helping you learn

Progress questions

1. What are the different ways of forming a question in the perfect tense?
2. Check your answer.

Discussion points

1. Discuss these different ways with fellow students and anyone interested in the subject.
2. Compare with ways of forming questions in the perfect tense in English.

Practical assignment

Translate some of the examples in English into French, using all three methods for each example.

Study tips

1. Read and re-read rules and appropriate examples (patterns) until you have absorbed the rules and patterns.
2. Little and often works well.

12

Negative and Near Negative Forms in the Perfect Tense

This chapter covers the complete list of negative forms. Each negative form consists of two words; the first of these is always *ne* (or *n'* in front of vowels and sometimes the letter 'h').

These two words fit around the verb in the imperfect tense; however, there are two word order patterns in the perfect tense.

■ *Not, no longer, never, not anything/nothing* and *hardly* surround the words added for auxiliary verb in the perfect tense:

Vous n'êtes pas arrivé tard.
You haven't arrived late/you didn't arrive late.

Elles n'ont pas réservé.
They haven't booked/they didn't book.

Tu n'as pas fait les lits?
You haven't made/you didn't make the beds?

Il n'a pas regardé le feuilleton.
He hasn't watched/he didn't watch the soap opera.

Je ne suis pas allé à l'église.
I haven't gone/I didn't go to church.

Tu n'as pas menti.
You haven't lied/you didn't lie.

Il n'a pas obéi.
He hasn't obeyed/he didn't obey.

Nous n'avons pas voté.
We haven't voted/we didn't vote.

Nous n'avons pas pu dépasser le fourgon.
We could not overtake the van.

Je n'ai pas eu le temps.
I did not have the time.

* * *

Vous n'êtes plus arrivé en retard?
Didn't you arrive late any more?

Elles n'ont plus réservé.
They didn't book any more.

Tu n'as plus fait les lits?
Didn't you make the beds any more?

Il n'a plus regardé les feuilletons.
He didn't watch the soaps any more.

Je ne suis plus allé à l'église.
I stopped/I did stop going to church.

Tu n'as plus menti?
You stopped/did you stop lying?

Il n'a plus obéi.
He stopped/he did stop obeying.

Nous n'avons plus voté.
We stopped/we did stop voting.

Je ne suis plus monté au village.
I stopped going up to the village.

Elle n'a plus fumé.
She stopped smoking.

* * *

Vous n'êtes jamais arrivé tard?
You have never arrived late?

Elles n'ont jamais réservé.
They have never booked.

Tu n'as jamais fait les lits?
You have never made the beds?

Il n'a jamais regardé les feuilletons.
He has never watched the soaps.

Je ne suis jamais allé à l'église.
I have never gone to church.

Tu n'as jamais menti?
You have never lied?

Il n'a jamais obéi.
He has never obeyed.

Nous n'avons jamais voté.
We have never voted.

Elle n'est jamais venue ici.
She has never come here.

On n'a jamais essayé.
We have never tried.

* * *

Elles n'ont rien réservé.
They haven't booked/they didn't book anything.

Tu n'as rien fait?
You haven't done/you didn't do anything?

Je n'ai rien trouvé.
I haven't found/I didn't find anything.

Il n'a rien regardé.
He hasn't watched/he didn't watch anything.

Elle n'a rien mangé.
He hasn't eaten/she didn't eat anything.

Vous n'avez rien compris?
You haven't understood/you didn't understand anything?

Ils n'ont rien vu.
They haven't seen/they didn't see anything.

Elle n'a rien acheté.
She hasn't bought/she didn't buy anything.

On a rien dit.
We haven't said/we didn't say anything.

Nous n'avons rien envoyé.
We haven't sent/we didn't send anything.

* * *

Je ne suis guère allé à l'église.
I have hardly (ever) gone to church.

On n'a guère vu le soleil!
We hardly saw the sun.

Elle n'a guère mangé.
She hardly ate anything.

Vous n'avez guère compris?
You hardly understood anything?

On n'a guère eu le temps.
We only just had the time.

Il n'a guère gelé cette année.
It scarcely snowed this year.

Je n'ai guère connu ton cousin.
I hardly knew your cousin.

Il n'y a guère eu de problèmes.
There have hardly been any problems.

Elle n'a guère donné d'explications.
She hardly explained anything.

Il n'y a guère eu de doutes.
There were hardly any uncertainties.

■ *Only, neither-nor/either-or, no-one/nobody, nowhere* and *no/none/not one* are placed before and after the whole compound verb in the perfect tense:

Je n'ai acheté que deux bouteilles.
I only bought/I have only bought two bottles.

Il n'a gelé qu'une fois cette année.
It only snowed/it has only snowed once this year.

Elle n'a cassé qu'une tasse.
She only broke/she has only broken one cup.

Il n'a maigri que de deux kilos.
He only lost/he has only lost two kilos.

Nous ne nous sommes occupés que des animaux.
We only looked after/we have only looked after the pets.

Je n'ai acheté que le persil.
I only bought/I have only bought the parsley.

Heureusement le car n'a heurté que le trottoir.
Fortunately the coach only hit/has only hit the pavement.

Ils n'ont bu que de l'eau.
They only drank water.

On n'a regardé que le sport.
We only watched sport.

Tu n'as dis que des bêtises.
You only said silly things.

NOTE: The use of the word 'Seulement' (an alternative way to say "only") can be placed after the first **or** the second part of the compound verb:

J'ai seulement acheté deux bouteilles
J'ai acheté seulement deux bouteilles
I only bought/I have only bought two bottles.

* * *

Il n'a appris ni l'italien ni l'allemand.
He has learnt neither Italian nor German.

Je n'ai habité ni à Nice ni à Cannes.
I haven't lived in Nice or in Cannes.

Ils n'ont joué ni avec le chat ni avec le chien.
They didn't play with the dog or with the cat.

Nous ne sommes allés ni en Italie, ni en Espagne.
We have been neither to Italy nor to Spain.

On n'a goûté ni la tarte ni la glace.
We tasted neither the tart nor the ice cream.

Vous n'avez vu ni Elise ni Elodie?
Haven't you seen Elise or Elodie?

Elle n'a acheté ni le pain ni le lait.
She bought neither the bread nor the milk.

Il n'a fait ni chaud ni froid.
It was neither hot nor cold.

Je n'ai choisi ni le potage ni les crudités.
I didn't choose the soup or the crudités.

Tu n'as aimé ni le potage ni la viande?
Didn't you like the soup or the meat?

* * *

Nous n'avons rencontré personne.
We haven't met/we didn't meet anyone.

Elle n'a remercié personne.
She hasn't thanked/she didn't thank anybody.

Il n'a regardé personne.
He hasn't looked/he didn't look at anybody.

Vous n'avez compris personne?
You didn't understand anyone?

Tu n'as parlé à personne?
You haven't spoken/you didn't speak to anyone?

On n'a dérangé personne.
We haven't disturbed/we didn't disturb anybody.

Ils n'ont cru personne.
They didn't believe anyone.

Il n' y a eu personne.
There hasn't been anybody.

Je n'ai trouvé personne.
I haven't found/I didn't find anybody.

Elle n'a aimé personne.
She didn't like anyone.

* * *

On n'a été nulle part le week-end dernier.
We didn't go anywhere last weekend.

Vous n'êtes allé nulle part alors?
So you didn't go anywhere?

Nous n'avons cherché nulle part pour le moment.
We haven't looked anywhere yet.

Il n'est allé nulle part ce dimanche-là.
He went nowhere that Sunday.

Tu ne t'es amusé nulle part alors?
So, you didn't have fun anywhere?

Heureusement, je ne me suis fait mal nulle part.
I did not hurt myself anywhere, fortunately.

Tu es sûr que tu n'as laissé ton sac nulle part dans la maison?
Are you sure that you haven't left your bag somewhere in
the house?

*Il n'a conduit nulle part pendant une heure, pour passer le
temps.*
He drove nowhere in particular for an hour, to kill time.

* * *

Il n'y a eu aucun risque.
There wasn't/there hasn't been any danger at all.

Je n'ai envoyé aucune lettre.
I haven't sent/I didn't send any letters whatsoever.

Nous n'avons touché aucun bibelot.
We haven't touched/we didn't touch a single ornament.

Vous n'avez visité aucun musée?
You haven't visited/you didn't visit one single museum?

Elles n'ont mangé aucune fois ici.
They haven't eaten here once.

Je n'ai entendu aucun bruit.
I haven't heard/I didn't hear a single sound.

Elle n'a chanté aucune de mes chansons préférées.
She did not sing a single song of the songs I like best.

Il n'a appris aucun mot français.
He hasn't learned/he didn't learn a single French word.

NOTE: There is a masculine and a feminine form for 'no/none/not one: aucun/aucune.' Note also that in <u>all</u> tenses, *ne* tends to be omitted in speech and in casual written French.

Helping you learn

Progress questions

1. What are the rules for negative forms in the perfect tense?
2. Check your answer.

Discussion points

Discuss rules for negative forms in the perfect tense with fellow students and anyone else interested in the subject.

Practical assignment

1. Translate some of the examples in English or in French.
2. Check your answers.

Study tips
Practice is the only secret to improving fluency.

13

Perfect or Present? Two Key Structures

As mentioned previously, it is only when using the 'depuis' and 'venir de' key structures that the perfect tense in English does not translate to the perfect tense in French.

■ To talk about things that people have been doing or to talk about the state of affairs up to and including the present moment, when an action or a situation is still in progress and therefore not finished, use 'depuis' (literally 'since') and the <u>present</u> tense:

On travaille dans le jardin depuis vingt minutes.
We have worked/have been working in the garden for twenty minutes.

Ils partagent une chambre depuis deux mois.
They have shared/have been sharing a bedroom for two months.

Quelqu'un frappe à la porte depuis cinq minutes.
Someone has been knocking at the door for five minutes.

Il pleut depuis trois jours.
It has been raining for three days.

Ils font le régime depuis cinq semaines.
They have been on a diet for five weeks.

Je m'inquiète depuis six heures.
I have been worrying since six o'clock.

Tu connais ce monsieur depuis combien de temps?
How long have you known this man?

Il habite ici depuis janvier.
He has lived here since January.

Il dort depuis cinq heures.
He has been asleep since five/for five hours.

Elle irrite son frère depuis ce matin.
She has been irritating her brother since this morning.

Il est mort depuis deux ans.
He has been dead for two years.

Ils sont divorcés depuis trois mois.
They have been divorced for three months.

Elle se repose depuis une heure.
She has been resting for an hour/since one o'clock.

Tu es végétarien depuis combien de temps?
How long have you been a vegetarian?

Ils pleurent depuis un bon moment.
They have been crying for ages.

Nous habitons ici depuis 1990.
We have lived/we have been living here since 1990.

Elle travaille depuis plusieurs heures.
She has worked for several hours.

Il a un chien depuis six mois.
He has had a dog for six months.

Nous sommes végétariens depuis 1989.
We have been vegetarians since 1989.

Vous êtes malade depuis trois jours?
You have been ill for three days?

Vous êtes ici depuis combien de temps?
How long have you been here?

Elles sont ici depuis janvier.
They have been here since January.

Tu as un ordinateur depuis longtemps?
Have you had a computer for a long time?

Il a une voiture depuis plusieurs mois.
He has had a car for several months.

Mes parents connaissent cette famille depuis très longtemps.
My parents have known this family for ages.

La voiture est au garage depuis mardi.
The car has been at the garage since Tuesday.

La ville est sans maire depuis un mois.
The town has been without a mayor for one month.

On regarde les canards depuis une heure.
We have been watching the ducks for one hour/since one o'clock.

Ils font le régime depuis cinq semaines.
They have been on a diet for five weeks.

Elles viennent ici depuis dix ans.
They have been coming here for ten years.

Les gosses s'amusent depuis deux heures.
The kids have been playing for two hours/since two o'clock.

Ils sont mariés depuis longtemps.
They have been married for a long time.

Elle flirte avec lui depuis ce matin.
She has been flirting with him since this morning.

Elles gardent nos chiens depuis lundi.
They have looked after our dogs since Monday.

Il y a la canicule depuis plusieurs jours.
There has been a heat wave for several days.

Ils mangent depuis ce matin.
They have been eating since this morning.

Ils habitent en France depuis 1992.
They have lived/have been living in France since 1992.

Il apprend le français depuis plusieurs mois maintenant.
He has been learning French for several months now.

Elle a de la fièvre depuis lundi.
She has had a temperature since Monday.

Nous sommes inquiets depuis hier soir.
We have been worrying since last night.

> ■ However, when describing an action or a state of affairs which had already started prior to another action or state of affairs in the past, and which was still in progress when this second action took place, the imperfect tense is used in French (not, as in English, the pluperfect):

Je travaillais à Nice depuis dix ans quand je suis tombé malade.
I had been working in Nice for ten years, when I fell ill.

*Vous possédiez une maison en France depuis longtemps
quand votre femme est morte?*
Had you owned a house in France for a long time when
your wife died?

*Ils étaient riches depuis seulement quelques mois quand cette
tragédie est survenue.*
They had been rich for only a few months when this
tragedy struck.

*On cherchait le chien depuis trois heures lorsque la police a
téléphoné.*
We had been looking for the dog for three hours/since three
o'clock when the police phoned.

*Il réparait le vélo depuis environ vingt minutes quand il a
entendu des cris dans la rue.*
He had been mending the bike for about twenty minutes
when he heard shouts in the street.

Tu étais malade depuis combien de temps quand c'est arrivé?
How long had you been ill for when that happened?

Elle habitait chez toi depuis quand lorsque ton fils est né?
She had lived with you for how long when your son was born?

Je promenais mon chien depuis une demi-heure quand il a commencé à neiger.
I had been walking my dog for half an hour when it started to snow.

On attendait la lettre depuis dix jours quand on a décidé de téléphoner.
We had been waiting for the letter for ten days when we decided to phone.

Ils connaissaient mon mari depuis des années.
They had known my husband for years.

Elle parlait depuis plus d'une demi-heure.
She had been speaking for more than half an hour.

Nous nous connaissions depuis pas mal de temps.
We had known each other for ages.

On écoutait ce feuilleton à la radio depuis des années.
We had been listening to this radio soap for years.

Ils conduisaient depuis deux heures à peu près.
They had been driving for about two hours/since about two o'clock.

Nous nous écrivions depuis notre enfance.
We had been writing to each other since our childhood.

Elle manquait d'argent depuis un an.
She had been short of money for a year.

Il regardait la télé depuis midi.
He had been watching TV since midday.

Nous habitions dans le village depuis 1999.
We had lived in the village since 1999.

Elle collectionnait les pièces depuis qu'elle avait dix ans.
She had been collecting coins since she was ten years old.

Ils ne conduisaient que depuis quelques minutes quand la voiture a fait un drôle de bruit.
They had only been driving a few minutes when the car made a strange noise.

> ■ To talk about what someone <u>has just done</u> (in the very recent past), use the present tense of '*venir*' together with '*de*' followed by the verb denoting the action or state of affairs in the infinitive:

Je viens de voir le facteur.
I have just seen the postman.

Tu viens de manquer ton copain.
You have just missed your friend.

Elle vient de finir.
She has just finished.

Il vient de tomber.
He has just fallen.

Nous venons de demander.
We have just asked.

Vous venez de prendre une douche?
Have you just had a shower?

Ils viennent d'arriver.
They have just arrived.

Je viens d'être malade.
I have just been ill.

On vient de se servir de la tondeuse.
We have just used the lawn mower.

Elle vient de compléter la feuille.
She has just filled in the form.

Le chien vient d'aboyer.
The dog has just barked.

Elle vient de partir.
She has just left.

Il vient d'envoyer un mél.
He has just sent an email.

On vient de manger.
We have just eaten.

Tu viens de laver la robe?
Have you just washed the dress?

Elles viennent d'acheter un appartement.
They have just bought a flat.

Je viens de laver la voiture.
I have just washed the car.

Tu viens de voir ton frère?
Have you just seen your brother?

Elle vient de partir.
She has just left.

On vient de se réveiller.
We have just woken up.

Vous venez d'envoyer la lettre?
Have you just sent the letter?

Ils viennent de quitter le bureau.
They have just left the office.

Nos enfants viennent de manger.
Our children have just eaten.

Elodie vient de téléphoner.
Elodie has just phoned.

Mon mari et moi venons de descendre.
My husband and I have just come downstairs.

Il vient d'écrire.
He has just written.

Son cheval vient de mourir.
His horse has just died.

Le bus vient d'arriver.
The bus has just arrived.

Notre fille vient de se lever.
Our daughter has just got up.

Je viens de prendre une tasse de café.
I have just had a cup of coffee.

Les enfants viennent de rentrer.
The children have just come in.

Tu viens de téléphoner?
Have you just phoned?

Je viens de payer l'addition.
I have just paid the bill.

Elle vient de refuser.
She has just refused.

Ils viennent de répondre.
They have just replied.

Tu viens de crier?
Have you just screamed?

Il vient de bouger.
He has just moved.

Je viens de vendre la voiture.
I have just sold the car.

Vous venez de voter?
Have you just voted?

C'est ce que je viens de dire.
That's what I have just said.

■ Similar to the *'depuis'* key structure above, when describing an action or state of affairs which had just taken place when another action or state of affairs arose, the imperfect tense is used in French (not, as in English, the pluperfect):

Elle venait de demander quand tu es arrivé.
She had just asked when you arrived.

Ils venaient de partir quand il a commencé à neiger.
They had just left when it started to snow.

Je venais d'arriver quand quelqu'un a sonné.
I had just arrived when someone rang the doorbell.

L'avion venait d'attérir quand il s'est évanoui.
The plane had just landed when he fainted.

Je venais de passer mon permis de conduire quand ma femme a accouché.
I had just taken my driving test when my wife gave birth to our baby.

Nous venions de la voir.
We had just seen her.

Il venait d'aller mieux.
He had just got better.

On venait d'écouter les actualités.
We had just been listening to the news.

Vous veniez de déménager?
You had just moved house?

Je venais de leur parler.
I had just spoken to them.

La maison venait d'être vendue.
The house had just been sold.

Elle venait de prendre un bain.
She had just had a bath.

Vous veniez de finir de faire le gâteau?
Had you just finished making the cake?

Il venait d'écrire.
He had just written.

On venait de manger.
We had just eaten.

Les chiens venaient d'aboyer.
The dogs had just barked.

Nous venions de répondre.
We had just answered.

Mes amis venaient de se marier.
My friends had just got married.

Il venait de pleuvoir.
It had just been raining.

Elles venaient de regarder le coucher de soleil.
They had just been watching the sunset.

Helping you learn

Progress questions

What are the two key structures that require the perfect tense in English but the present tense in French?

Discussion points

Discuss these key structures with fellow students and anyone else interested in the subject.

Practical assignment

Translate some of the English and some of the French examples.

Study tips
Never miss an opportunity to use your French.

14

Three More Past Tenses

The past historic replaces the perfect tense mostly in formal written French and in novels.

As useful as the perfect and the imperfect tenses in everyday conversation are the pluperfect and the subjunctive perfect. Usage of these two tenses does not generally cause the same initial problems as the perfect and imperfect tenses seem to give. Once the perfect and imperfect tenses are understood, the pluperfect could not be more straightforward. As for the subjunctive perfect (a tense that has more or less disappeared in spoken English), although rules for usage can be found in grammar books, my advice is to practice the language as much as possible and completely immerse yourself in it; usage will become automatic through sheer repetition.

■ The Past Historic

➤ As mentioned previously, the past historic (*passé simple*) is never used in spoken French or in letters. It replaces the perfect tense in books and in formal written texts such as newspaper articles. As a formal tense used for narration, the past historic is mainly used with the third person forms: *he*, *she*, *it*, *they* and *this* or *that*.

➤ There are three sets of endings:

Je	ai	is	us
Tu	as	is	us
Il/Elle/On	a	it	ut
Nous	âmes	îmes	ûmes
Vous	âtes	îtes	ûtes
Ils/Elles	èrent	irent	urent

> ➤ Generally, recognising the verb is not a problem:

Elles finirent à dix heures.
They finished at ten.

Ils conduisirent.
They drove.

Elles étonnèrent tout le monde.
They surprised everybody.

On alla au port.
We went to the harbour.

Cela parut inutile.
It seemed pointless.

Elle descendit.
She went down.

Ils mangèrent dans la cuisine.
They ate in the kitchen.

Ils déménagèrent en '85.
They moved house in '85.

On loua un studio.
We rented a studio.

Ils essayèrent.
They tried.

Elle partit.
She left.

Ceci produisit un résultat surprenant.
It gave a surprising result.

Cela créa des désavantages.
That created some drawbacks.

Elles décidèrent de venir.
They decided to come.

Il compta les billets.
He counted the tickets.

Ils se demandèrent pourquoi.
They wondered why.

Elle donna l'argent.
She gave the money.

Vous parlâtes longtemps?
Did you speak for a long time?

Je vendis la maison.
I sold the house.

Nous nous lavâmes.
We washed.

Vous voulûtes voir?
Did you want to see?

Nous réservâmes une table pour 8 heures.
We booked a table for eight.

Tu voulus rester?
Did you want to stay?

Nous arrivâmes très tôt.
We arrived early.

J'écrivis à ma marraine.
I wrote to my Godmother.

> ➤ However, the four very useful verbs given below – 'to
> be,' 'to have,' 'to make/to do' and 'to be able to' are not
> as easily recognisable.

ETRE	AVOIR	FAIRE	POUVOIR
Je fus	J'eus	Je fis	Je pus
Tu fus	Tu eus	Tu fis	Tu pus
Il/Elle/On fut	Il/Elle/On eut	Il/Elle/On fit	Il/Elle/On put
Nous fûmes	Nous eûmes	Nous fîmes	Nous pûmes
Vous fûtes	Vous eûtes	Vous fîtes	Vous pûtes
Ils/Elles furent	Ils/Elles eurent	Ils/Elles firent	Ils/Elles purent

■ Pluperfect Tense

➢ The pluperfect is used when talking about events in the past that had taken place before other past events had occurred i.e. when referring to about past events which preceded others. It is also the tense used for reporting speech that was originally either in the imperfect or in the perfect tense.

➢ The auxiliary verbs, *avoir* or *être*, are in the imperfect. Past participles are the same as for the perfect tense.

J'avais vu le docteur.
I had seen the doctor.

Tu avais terminé?
Had you finished?

Ils s'étaient excusés.
They had apologised.

La voiture avait été réparée la veille.
The car had been mended the day before.

Le chien avait attaqué l'enfant.
The dog had attacked the child.

Nous avions réfléchi pendant toute la semaine.
We had given it some thought the whole week.

Elle était allée à Paris.
She had gone to Paris.

On avait acheté les légumes.
We had bought some vegetables.

Il y avait eu un problème trois jours avant.
There had been a problem three days before.

Vous vous étiez levé avant huit heures?
Had you got up before eight?

Ils étaient montés dans le grenier.
They had gone up to the loft.

J'étais sortie.
I had gone out.

Elles avaient voulu attendre.
They had wanted to wait.

J'avais entendu.
I had heard.

On avait refusé.
We had refused.

Il avait nettoyé le four.
He had cleaned the oven.

J'étais tombé.
I had fallen.

Tu étais parti?
Had you left?

Elles avaient compris la situation.
They had understood the situation.

On avait mangé du poulet.
We had eaten some chicken.

Vous aviez dépensé beaucoup d'argent?
Had you spent a lot of money?

Il avait fait très froid.
It had been very cold.

Nous avions hésité.
We had hesitated.

Elle s'était habillée rapidement.
She had dressed quickly.

Le camion avait klaxonné deux fois.
The lorry had hooted twice.

■ The Perfect Subjunctive

➢ The subjunctive is used to express emotions, such as fears, doubts and wishes. It is used to express possibilities and necessities. This tense is also needed after a superlative and after certain conjunctions. (It is more or less impossible to translate this tense literally. There is no direct equivalent in English, as this tense has almost disappeared in this language.)

➤ The perfect subjunctive is formed using the present subjunctive of *être* and *avoir*:

	AVOIR	ÊTRE
Je-J'	aie	sois
Tu	aies	sois
Il/Elle/On	ait	soit
Nous	ayons	soyons
Vous	ayez	soyez
Ils/Elles	aient	soient

➤ Past participles remain the same as for the perfect tense:

J'aurais préféré que vous soyez resté un autre jour.
I would have preferred it if you had stayed one more day.

Elle est restée jusqu'à ce que j'aie téléphoné.
She stayed until I phoned.

Nous aurions voulu qu'il ait terminé ses études.
We would have liked him to finish his studies.

Ils sont partis avant que tu aies pu leur parler?
Did they go before you were able to speak to them?

Nous sommes contents que vous soyez venus.
We are pleased that you have come.

Il est possible qu'ils aient acheté un camping-car.
It is possible that they have bought a motorhome.

C'est le film le plus émouvant que nous ayons vu.
It is the most moving film that we have seen.

Il faut qu'elle ait passé son permis de conduire.
She needs to have passed her driving test.

Nous avions peur qu'ils ne se soient perdus.
We got worried that they had got lost.

Il aurait été préférable que vous ayez dit la vérité tout de suite.
It would have been better for you to tell the truth straight away.

Il est possible que nous ayons eu raison.
It is possible that we were right.

Il m'a tenu compagnie jusqu'à ce que le train soit arrivé.
He stayed with me until the train arrived.

Quoi que vous ayez fait, cela n'a aucune importance maintenant.
Whatever you have done, it is not important at all now.

Bien que nous ayons payé, on nous a refusé l'entrée.
Although we paid, they refused to let us in.

Il semblerait qu'il y ait eu une erreur.
It would seem that there has been a mistake.

Elle n'aurait pas aimé que tu aies été en retard.
She would not have liked it if you had been late.

On avait attendu pour qu'elle ait pu finir.
We had waited so that she could finish.

Tu aurais souhaité que je sois allée chez le docteur aujourd'hui?
Would you have preferred that I had gone to the doctor today?

Bien que nous ayons perdu, nous nous sommes bien amusés.
Although we lost we really enjoyed ourselves.

Elle leur pardonnera, quoiqu'elles aient fait.
She will forgive them whatever they may have done.

On doutait que vous ayez trouvé la solution.
We doubted that you had found the solution.

Quoique que nous ayons dit, cela n'aurait rien changé.
Whatever we could have said would not have made a difference.

Il faut que tu aies terminé avant huit heures.
You have to finish before eight.

Je suis désolé que tu aies eu tant de problèmes.
I am sorry that you have had so many problems.

Il est regrettable qu'il ait entendu ça.
It is unfortunate that he heard that.

Helping you learn

Progress questions

1. What are the other three past tenses covered in this chapter?
2. How are they formed?

Discussion points

Discuss and compare past tenses in French and in English with fellow students and anyone else interested in the subject.

Practical assignment

Translate some of the French and English examples.

Study tips
Practice, practice, practice.

15 Grammatical Terms

One-minute overview

This short closing section explains an absolute minimum of the most commonly used grammatical terms that are useful for the material in *Better French 2*. Clear definitions of these grammatical terms are given in English, with illustrating examples in English. This section could be completely ignored by some learners, but it may prove useful to others.

A **subject** is the doer of the verb (noun or pronoun):

I have eaten.
You ran all the way?
These sweets are expensive.
We have decided.
The train arrived early.
The potatoes have rotted.
He has always enjoyed good health.
A solution was found.
Problems have come up.
My husband liked the French dish.
It snowed.
The house was old.
His friends used to have a French car.
The house was expensive.
Their ceiling collapsed.

A **noun** is a **person**, an **animal**, a **place** or a **thing** (including abstract things). All French nouns are either masculine or feminine:

My **niece**, the **cats**, the **beach**, this **idea**, **grass**, our **caravan**, a **tree**, **friends**, the **teacher**, the **lift**, an **apple**, his **toys**, this **village**, her **brother**, your **country**, the **birds**, your **opinion**, some **beer**, **love**, a **month**, two **cups**, some **money**, several **difficulties**, some **shoes**, **patience**.

A pronoun is a word that replaces a noun. In particular pronouns replace nouns previously mentioned, in order to avoid repetition and shorten sentences:

The boys have washed the **socks**. **They** have washed **them**.
My uncle has written **a letter**. **He** has written **it**.
Has **Stephanie** bought **the croissants**? Has **she** bought **them**?
Has **her husband** met **my Godson**? Has **he** met **him**?
The women have made **the cakes**. **They** have made **them**.
Her dog has broken **the plates**. **He** has broken **them**.
My grandparents knew **your sister** well? **They** knew **her** well?
The police showed **the photographs** to **the teacher**. **They** showed **them** to **him**.
The manager talked to **us**. **He** talked to **us**.
They have described **the house** to **my mother**. **They** have described **it** to **her**.
We have discovered **the secret** of the recipe. **We** have discovered **it**.
Did **you** choose **the bouillabaisse**? Did **you** choose **it**?
We lent **the book** to **your friend** last week. **We** lent **it** to **him** last week.
She received **the invoices**. **She** received **them**.
Has **he** spoken to **the waiter**? Has **he** spoken to **him**?
We showed the present to our children. **We** showed **it** to **them**.
Has **the man** advised **your husband** to phone? Has **he** advised **him** to phone?
I have cut **the cake**. **I** have cut **it**.
The locals have known **us** for years. **They** have known **us** for years.
They have seen **me**.

A reflexive verb is a verb whose action reflects back on the subject. These take reflexive pronouns: myself, yourself, yourselves, oneself, himself, herself, itself, ourselves, themselves, (the plural forms double for 'one another' or 'each other'). There are more reflexive verbs in French than there are in English.

An auxiliary verb is a verb that is needed in certain constructions, a verb that accompanies particular forms of a main verb to express a tense, a verb that supports the key verb. The two auxiliary verbs used in this book are *être* (**to be**) and *avoir* (**to have**).

A direct object is a noun or pronoun that receives the action of a verb, or that is affected by the action of the verb:

She knew **my uncle**. She knew **him**.
We sang **a song**. We sang **it**.
The ring (that) I lost was quite old.
They liked **you**.
I have made **the sandwiches**. I have made **them**.
He sent a **postcard**. He sent **it**.
He has left **me**.
Have you bought **the newspapers**? Have you bought **them**?
We saw **Caroline**. We saw **her**.
The disks (that) I have chosen are on the table.
I have met **your parents**. I have met **them**.
Have you seen **Claude**? Have you seen **him**?
They have helped **us**.
The car (that) we have sold was white.
They looked at **the little girl**. They looked at **her**.
We ate **the pizza**. We ate **it**.
My mother bought **the shoes**. She bought **them**.
The house (that) we chose is fifty years old.
The neighbours saw **us**.
I left **the box** in the bedroom. I left **it** in the bedroom.
She hated **the present**. She hated **it**.
We mended **the chairs**. We mended **them**.
They encouraged **their children**. They encouraged **them**.
You heard **the thunder**? You heard **it**?
They have forgotten **their bags**. They have forgotten **them**.

An indirect object is a noun or pronoun governed by a preposition, that is therefore <u>indirectly</u> affected by the action of the verb:

He spoke **to the man**.
The children have described the school **to their grandparents**. The children have described the school **to them**.
He feeds the carrots **to the donkeys**. He feeds the carrots **to them**.
We have written **to you**.
She sang **us** a song. She sang a song **to us**.
They gave **me** a box of chocolates. They gave a box of chocolates **to me**.
She showed **my daughter** the house. She showed the house **to her**.
I described the man **to the police**. I described the man **to them**.
He sent the letter **to me**.
Have you replied **to your parents**?

A transitive verb is a verb that expresses an action that is carried from a subject to an object, and so requires a direct object:

I **liked** the film.
Have you **defrosted** the meat?
We **bought** the beer.
She **missed** the boat.
They **made** a cake.
She **found** the books.
Did you **choose** the curtains?
They **hired** a flat.
He **ate** a pizza.
She **won** the race.
We have **paid** the bill.
She **had** a baby.
They **cancelled** the party.
Who **painted** the walls?
He **broke** a bottle.

However, some transitive verbs can also be used intransitively:

Where did they **eat**?

He **ate** at one o'clock.

I never **win**.
She **won** yesterday.

An intransitive verb is a verb that does not require a direct object to complete its meaning:

He **died**.
They **became angry**.
She **swam** for an hour.
It **rained**.
We **talked**.
Did they **sleep** well?
Where did you **fall**?
I **went** to France.
They **woke up** late.
She **came** last night.
They **were right**.
I had **to phone**.
I **was able to** do it.
They **reacted** badly.
They **ran** fast.

Agreement is when a word (in this book the past participle) has to match who or what it refers to in both gender and number. French has masculine, feminine, singular and plural forms.

An 'e' is added to mark the feminine. Adding this 'e' only affects the pronunciation of past participles ending in a consonant. In this case, the word has an extra syllable, for example '*fait*' from '*faire*' (to make, to do), or '*compris*' from '*comprendre*' (to understand) in the feminine form become '*faite*' and '*comprise*' respectively.

An 's' is added to mark the plural (this is not pronounced). When 's' is actually the last letter of the past participle, for example '*mis*' from '*mettre*' (to put) or '*surpris*' from '*surprendre*' (to take by surprise, to catch) there is no change in the plural form.

Web sites and useful Addresses

www.alliancefr.org
L'Alliance Française, home page of the leading French cultural and language teaching organisation, with branches worldwide.

www.hachette.com
Books, dictionaries publishers.

http://www.icicampus.com/
Guide internet pour étudiants (études, cours, formation, écoles et universités).

www.fuaj.org/fra/
National Youth Hostel centre.

www.tourisme.fr
National French tourist office.

http://www.parisinfo.com
Hotels, restaurants, visits, events, museum, monuments, night life in Paris.

www.v1.paris.fr/EN
Information on sights, museums, parks, cemeteries, city government and studying or living in Paris.

http://www.librairieonline.com/tg/
French supplier of books, videos, Cds and other products online.

http://www.parismatch.com/
Monthly news magazine

http://www.lemonde.fr
Left-wing newspaper.

http://www.lefigaro.fr/
Right-wing newspaper.

www.lequipe.fr/
Sport news.

http://www.meteofrance.com/FR/index.jsp
Weather forecast service.

http://fr.yahoo.com/
French search engine.

www.bbc.co.uk/languages

www.frenchentree.com/
The guide to property, holidays and life in France.

http://www.frenchentree.com/languedoc-herault-gard-french-language-learning/
Learning French in the South of France, and more.

www.bonjourdefrance.com
Le magazine pour pratiquer le français et dialoguer sur internet.

www.french-news.com/
France's English-language monthly newspaper.

www.francemag.com
Monthly English-language review of la vie française with a world-wide following. Ususally includes a language page.

www.livingfrance.com
Monthly magazine in English, exclusively devoted to France and all things French. Ususally includes some French for learning purposes.

www.french-property-news.com/
Monthly magazine in English, aimed at buyers of property in France. Ususally includes some French for learning purposes.

www.hadleypager.com
Series of books for the English-French and French-English market.

www.concordefrench.com
8 Skye Close
Maidstone
Kent ME15 9SJ
Tel: 01622 749167
Fax: 01622 744508
Monthly magazines in French for UK readers.

www.aufildesmots.co.uk
aufildesmotsltd@btconnect.com
Au Fil des Mots
French bookshop
19 Bute Street (less than 2 minutes walk from South Kensington tube station)
London SW7 3EY
Tel/Fax: 0207 589 9400

www.frenchbookshop.com
info@frenchbookshop.com
The French Bookshop
28 Bute Street
London SW7 3EX
Tel: 020 7584 2840
Fax: 020 7823 9259
French literature, magazines, CD Roms, including teaching material.

www.ambafrance-uk.org
French Embassy in the UK
58 Knightsbridge

London SW1X 7JT
Tel: 207 073 1000

www.consulfrance-londres.org
Consulat de France
21 Cromwell Road
London SW7 2EN

Index